HANDBOOKS FOR TH
CRAFTSMAN

Intarsia and Marquetry

BY

F. HAMILTON JACKSON

Examiner to the Board of Education in Principles
of Ornament

*With Illustrations from Photographs and from Drawings
and Tracings by the Author*

1903

British Library Cataloguing-in-Publication Data
A catalogue record for this book is available from the
British Library

Decorative Woodwork

Woodworking is the process of making items from wood. Along with stone, mud and animal parts, wood was one of the first materials worked by early humans. There are incredibly early examples of woodwork, evidenced in Mousterian stone tools used by Neanderthal man, which demonstrate our affinity with the wooden medium. In fact, the very development of civilisation is linked to the advancement of increasingly greater degrees of skill in working with these materials.

Examples of Bronze Age wood-carving include tree trunks worked into coffins from northern Germany and Denmark and wooden folding-chairs. The site of Fellbach-Schmieden in Germany has provided fine examples of wooden animal statues from the Iron Age. Woodworking is depicted in many ancient Egyptian drawings, and a considerable amount of ancient Egyptian furniture (such as stools, chairs, tables, beds, chests) has been preserved in tombs. The inner coffins found in the tombs were also made of wood. The metal used by the Egyptians for woodworking tools was originally copper and eventually, after 2000 BC, bronze - as ironworking was unknown until much later. Historically, woodworkers relied upon the woods native to their region, until transportation and trade innovations made more exotic woods available to the craftsman.

Today, often as a contemporary artistic and 'craft' medium, wood is used both in traditional and modern styles; an excellent material for delicate as well as forceful artworks. Wood is used in forms of sculpture, trade, and decoration including chip carving, wood burning, and marquetry, offering a fascination, beauty, and complexity in the grain that often shows even when the medium is painted. It is in some ways easier to shape than harder substances, but an artist or craftsman must develop specific skills to carve it properly. 'Wood carving' is really an entire genre itself, and involves cutting wood generally with a knife in one hand, or a chisel by two hands - or, with one hand on a chisel and one hand on a mallet. The phrase may also refer to the finished product, from individual sculptures to hand-worked mouldings composing part of a tracery.

The making of sculpture in wood has been extremely widely practiced but survives much less well than the other main materials such as stone and bronze, as it is vulnerable to decay, insect damage, and fire. It therefore forms an important hidden element in the arts and crafts history of many cultures. Outdoor wood sculptures do not last long in most parts of the world, so that we have little idea how the totem pole tradition developed. Many of the most important sculptures of China and Japan in particular are in wood, and the great majority of African sculptures and that of Oceania also use this medium. There are various forms of carving which can be utilised; 'chip carving' (a style of carving in which knives or chisels are used to remove small chips of the material), 'relief carving' (where figures are carved in a flat panel of wood), 'Scandinavian flat-plane' (where figures are carved in large flat planes, created primarily using a carving knife - and rarely rounded or sanded afterwards) and 'whittling' (simply carving shapes using just a knife). Each of these techniques will need slightly varying tools, but broadly speaking, a specialised 'carving knife' is essential, alongside a 'gouge' (a tool with a curved cutting edge used in a variety of forms and sizes for carving hollows, rounds and sweeping curves), a 'chisel' and a 'coping saw' (a small saw, used to cut off chunks of wood at once).

Although this is probably the most ancient, and still the most widely practiced form of decorative woodwork, there remains several other popular techniques. Working with veneer is relatively common - and in woodworking, 'veneer' refers specifically to thin slices of wood, usually thinner than 3 mm (1/8 inch), glued onto core panels (typically, wood, particle board or medium-density fiberboard) to produce flat panels such as doors, tops and panels for cabinets, parquet floors and parts of furniture. Veneer is obtained either by 'peeling' the trunk of a tree or by slicing large rectangular blocks of wood known as flitches. There are three main types of veneer-making equipment used commercially: A rotary lathe in which the wood is turned against a very sharp blade and peeled off in one continuous or semi-continuous roll. A slicing machine in which the flitch or piece of log is raised and lowered against the blade and slices of the log are made. And last but not least, a half-round lathe in which the log or piece of log can be turned and moved in such a way as to expose the most interesting parts of the grain.

Each slicing processes gives a very distinctive type of grain, depending upon the tree species. In any of the veneer-slicing methods, when the veneer is sliced, a distortion of the grain occurs. As it hits the wood, the knife blade creates a 'loose' side where the cells have been opened up by the blade, and a 'tight' side. The technique of using veneer is additionally used in Marquetry; more particularly the art and craft of applying pieces of veneer to a structure to form decorative patterns, designs or pictures. The technique may be applied to case furniture or even seat furniture, to decorative small objects with smooth, veneerable surfaces or to freestanding pictorial panels appreciated in their own right. Parquetry is similar in technique to marquetry; in the former the pieces of veneer are of simple repeating geometric shapes, forming tiling patterns such as would cover a floor (*parquet*), or forming basketweave or brickwork patterns, trelliswork and the like.

Marquetry (and parquetry too) again differ from the more ancient craft of inlay, or intarsia, in which a solid body of one material is cut out to receive sections of another to form the surface pattern. The word derives from a Middle French word meaning 'inlaid work'. The veneers used are primarily woods, but may include bone, ivory, turtle-shell (conventionally called 'tortoiseshell'), mother-of-pearl, pewter, brass or fine metals. Marquetry using coloured straw was a specialty of some European spa resorts from the end of the eighteenth century. Many exotic woods as well as common European varieties can be employed, from the near-white of boxwood to the near-black of ebony, with veneers that retain stains well, like sycamore, dyed to provide colours not found in nature. Marquetry as a modern craft most commonly uses knife-cut veneers. However, the knife-cutting technique usually requires a lot of time. For that reason, many marquetarians have switched to fret (an interlaced decorative design that is either carved in low relief on a solid background, or cut out with a fretsaw, coping saw, jigsaw or scroll saw) techniques.

As is evident from this brief historical and practical overview of decorative woodwork, it is an incredibly varied and exciting genre of arts and crafts; an ancient tradition still relevant in the modern day. Woodworkers range from hobbyists, individuals operating from the home environment, to artisan professionals with specialist workshops, and eventually large-scale factory operations. We hope the reader is inspired by this book to create some woodwork of their own.

CONTENTS

LIST OF ILLUSTRATIONS

GENERAL PREFACE TO THE SERIES

If there is one quality which more than another marks the demand of the present day it is the requirement of novelty. In every direction the question which is asked is not, "Is this fresh thing good? Is it appropriate to, and well-fitted for, its intended uses?" but "Is it novel?" And the constant change of fashion sets a premium upon the satisfaction of this demand and enlists the commercial instinct on the side of perpetual change. While there are directions in which this desire is not altogether harmful, since at least many monstrosities offend our eyes but for a short time, a full compliance with it by the designer is likely to prove disastrous to his reputation, and recent phases in which an attempt has been made to throw aside as effete and outworn the forms which have gradually grown with the centuries, and to produce something entirely fresh and individual, have shown how impossible it is at this period of the world's history to dispense with tradition, and, escaping from the accumulated experience of the race, set forth with childlike *naïveté*. Careful study of these experiments discloses the fact that in as far as they are successful in proportion and line they approach the successes of previous generations, and that the undigested use of natural *motifs* results not in nourishment but in nightmare.

The object aimed at by this series of handbooks is the recall of the designer and craftsman to a saner view of what constitutes originality by setting before them something of the experience of past times, when craft tradition was still living and the designer had a closer contact with the material in which his design was carried out than is usual at present. Since both design and craftsmanship as known until the end of the 18th century were the outcome of centuries of experience of the use of material and of the endeavour to meet daily requirements, it may be justly called folly to cast all this aside as the fripperies of bygone fashion which cramp the efforts of the designer, and attempt to start afresh without a rag of clothing, even if it were possible. At the same time it is not intended to advocate the direct copyism of any style, whether regarded as good, bad, or indifferent. Some minds find inspiration in the contemplation of natural objects, while others find the same stimulus in the works of man. The fashion of present opinion lays great stress upon the former source of inspiration, and considers the latter heretical, while, with a strange inconsistency, acclaiming a form of design based upon unnatural contortions of growth, and a treatment which is often alien to the material. It is the hope of the author to assist the second class of mind to the rivalling of the ancient glories of design and craftsmanship, and perhaps even to convert some of those whose talents are at present wasted in the chase of the will-o'-the-wisp of fancied novelty and individuality. Much of what appears to the uneducated and ill-informed talent as new is really but the re-discovery of *motifs* which have been tried and abandoned by bygone masters as unsuitable, and a greater acquaintance with their triumphs is likely, one would hope, to lead students, whether designers or craftsmen, to view with disgust undigested designs indifferently executed which have little but a fancied novelty to recommend them.

It is intended that each volume shall contain an historical sketch of the phase of design and craft treated of, with examples of the successful overcoming of the difficulties to be encountered in its practice, workshop recipes, and the modes of producing the effects required, with a chapter upon the limitations imposed by the material and the various modes of evading those limitations adopted by those who have not frankly accepted them.

PREFACE

The subject treated of in this handbook has, until lately, received scant attention in England; and except for short notices of a general nature contained in such books as Waring's "Arts Connected with Architecture," technical descriptions, such as those in Holtzapffel's "Turning and Mechanical Manipulation," and a few fugitive papers, has not been treated in the English language. On the Continent it has, however, been the subject of considerable research, and in Italy, Germany, and France books have been published which either include it as part of the larger subject of furniture, or treat in considerable detail instances of specially-important undertakings. From these various sources I have endeavoured to gather as much information as possible without too wearying an insistence upon unimportant details, and now present the results of my selection for the consideration of that part of the public which is interested in the handicrafts which merge into art, and especially for the designer and craftsman, whose business it is or may be to produce such works in harmonious co-operation in the present day, as they often did in days gone by, and, it may be hoped, with a success akin to that attained in those periods to which we look back as the golden age of art.

The books from which I have drawn my information are principally the following:—

In Italian—Borghese and Banchi's "Nuovi documenti per la storia dell' Arte Senese"; Brandolese's "Pitture, sculture, &c., di Padova"; Caffi's "Dei lavori d'intaglio in legname e d'intarsia nel Cattedrale di Ferrara"; Calvi's "Dei professori de belle arti che fiorirono in Milano ai tempi dei Visconti, &c."; Saba Castiglione's "Ricordi"; Erculei's paper in his "Catalogue of the Exhibition of works of carving and inlay held at Rome in 1885"; Finocchietti's "Report on carving and inlaid work in the Jurors' report on the Exhibition of 1867 in Paris"; Lanzi's "History of Painting in Italy"; Locatelli's "Iconografia Italiana"; Marchese's "Lives of Dominican Artists"; Milanesi's "Documenti per la Storia dell' Arte Senese"; Morelli's "Notizie d'opere di disegno nella prima metà dell' Secolo XVI."; Tassi's "Vite di pittori, architetti, &c., Bergamaschi"; Temanza's "Vite dei piu celebri architetti, &c., Dominicani"; Tiraboschi's "Biblioteca Modenese"; Della Valle's "Lettere Senesi sopra le belle Arti"; Vasari's "Lives," with Milanesi's notes and corrections, and papers in the "Bullettino di Arti, Industrie e Curiosità Veneziane," the "Atti e memorie della Società Savonese," the "Archivio Storico dell' Arte and its continuation as L'Arte," and the "Archivio Storico Lombardo," by such men as Michele Caffi, G. M. Urb, Ottavio Varaldo, Francesco Malaguzzi Valeri and L. T. Belgrano.

In German—Becker and Hefner Alteneck's "Kunstwerke and Geräths Schaften des Mittelalters und der Renaissance"; Bucher's "Geschichte der Technischen Kunst"; Burckhardt's "Additions to Kugler's Geschichte der Baukunst, and Geschichte der Renaissance in Italien"; Demmin's "Studien über die Stofflich-bildenden Künste"; Von Falke's "Geschichte des deutsches Kunstgewerbes"; Scherer's "Technik und Geschichte der Intarsia"; Schmidt's "Schloss Gottorp"; Seeman's "Kunstgewerbliche Handbücher"; Teirich's "Ornamente aus der Blüthezeit italienischer Renaissance," and articles in "Blätter für Kunstgewerbe," and the "Kunstgewerbeblatt of the Zeitschrift für bildende Kunst," by such men as Teirich, Issel and Ilg.

In French—Asselineau's "A. Boulle, ébéniste de Louis 14"; Burckhardt's "Le Cicerone"; Champeaux's "Le bois appliquée au mobilier," and "Le meuble"; Demmin's "Encyclopédie historique, archeologique, &c."; Luchet's "L'Arte industriel à l'Exposition Universelle de 1867," and other encyclopædias.

In English—"The handmaid to the arts"; Holtzapffel's "Turning and mechanical manipulation"; Pollen's paper on "Furniture in the Kensington Catalogue of Ancient and Modern furniture"; Leader Scott's "The Cathedral builders"; Tomlinson's "Cyclopædia of Useful Arts"; Waring's "The Arts connected with architecture"; and Digby Wyatt's "Industrial Arts of the 19th Century," together with detached articles found in various publications.

Those who desire further examples of arabesque patterns may find them in Issel's "Wandtäfelungen und Holzdecken"; Lacher's "Mustergültige holzintarsien der

Deutschen Renaissance aus dem 16 und 17 Jahrhundert"; Lachner's "Geschichte der Holzbaukunst in Deutschland"; Lichtwark's "Der ornamentstich der deutschen Frührenaissance"; Meurer's "Italienische Flachornamente aus der Zeit der Renaissance"; Teirich's "Ornamente aus der Blüthezeit italienischer Renaissance," and Rhenius "Eingelegte Holzornamente der Renaissance in Schlesien von 1550-1650."

I have thought it better to run the risk of incompleteness than to overload the text with the mere names of indifferent designers and craftsmen about whom and whose work scarcely anything is known, believing that my object would be attained more surely by pointing to the work and lives of those about whose capacity there can be no question.

My thanks are due to the officials of the British Museum Library and of the Art Library at the Victoria and Albert Museum for the great assistance which they have given me in many ways, the facilities afforded me, and their unfailing kindness and courtesy; and to the Director of the Victoria and Albert Museum for similar kindness and assistance.

I have also to thank my friend Mr. C. Bessant, whose experience in all kinds of cabinet work is so great, for very kindly looking over the section dealing with the processes of manufacture.

F. Hamilton Jackson.

INTARSIA AND MARQUETRY

HISTORICAL NOTES—ANTIQUITY

The word "intarsia" is derived from the Latin "interserere," to insert, according to the best Italian authorities, though Scherer says there was a similar word, "Tausia," which was applied to the inlaying of gold and silver in some other metal, an art practised in Damascus, and thence called damascening; and that at first the two words meant the same thing, but after a time one was applied to work in wood and the other to metal work. In the "Museo Borbonico," xii., p. 4, xv., p. 6, the word "Tausia" is said to be of Arabic origin, and there is no doubt that the art is Oriental. It perhaps reached Europe either by way of Sicily or through the Spanish Moors. "Marquetry," on the other hand, is a word of much later origin, and comes from the French "marqueter," to spot, to mark; it seems, therefore, accurate to apply the former term to those inlays of wood in which a space is first sunk in the solid to be afterwards filled with a piece of wood (or sometimes some other material) cut to fit it, and to use the latter for the more modern practice of cutting several sheets of differently-coloured thin wood placed together to the same design, so that by one cutting eight or ten copies of different colours may be produced which will fit into each other, and only require subsequent arranging and glueing, as well as for the more artistic effects of the marquetry of the 17th and 18th centuries, which were produced with similar veneers. The process of inlaying is of the most remote antiquity, and the student may see in the cases of the British Museum, at the Louvre, and in other museums, examples of both Assyrian and Egyptian inlaid patterns of metal and ivory, or ebony or vitreous pastes, upon both wood and ivory, dating from the 8th and 10th centuries before the Christian Era, or earlier. The Greeks and Romans also made use of it for costly furniture and ornamental sculpture; in Book 23 of the "Odyssey," Ulysses, describing to Penelope the bride-bed which he had made, says—"Beginning from this head-post, I wrought at the bedstead till I had finished it, and made it fair with inlaid work of gold, and of silver, and of ivory"; the statue and throne of Jupiter at Olympia had ivory, ebony, and many other materials used in its construction, and the chests in which clothes were kept, mentioned by Homer, were some of them ornamented with inlaid work in the precious metals and ivory. Pausanias describes the box of Kypselos, in the opisthodomos of the Temple of Hera, at Olympia, as elliptical in shape, made of cedar wood and adorned with mythological representations, partly carved in wood and partly inlaid with gold and ivory, in five strips which encircled the whole box, one above another. The Greek words for inlaying used by Homer and Pindar are "δαιδάλλω" and "κολλάω," and their derivatives, the first being also used for embroidering; Homer and Hesiod also use "ποικίλος" for "inlaid," which shows how closely at that time the arts were interwoven. These words have left no trace in the later terms, though κολλάω means to fix together, or to glue, and it is tempting to connect the French word "coller" with it.

Vitruvius and Pliny use the words "cerostrata" or "celostrata," which means, strictly speaking, "inlaid with horn," and "xilostraton." The woods used by the Greeks were ebony, cypress, cedar, oak, "sinila," yew, willow, lotus (celtis australis), and citron (thuyia cypressoides), a tree which grew on the slopes of the Atlas mountains. The value of large slabs of this last was enormous. Pliny says that Cicero, who was not very wealthy according to Roman notions, spent 500,000 sesterces (about £5400) for one table. Asinius Pollio spent £10,800, King Juba £13,050, and the family of the Cethegi £15,150 for a single slab. The value of this wood consisted chiefly in the beautiful lines of the veins and fibres; when they ran in wavy lines they were called "tigrinæ," tiger tables; when they formed spirals like so many little whirlpools they were called "pantherinæ," or panther tables, and when they had undulating, wavy marks like the filaments of a feather, especially if resembling the eyes on a peacock's tail, they were very highly esteemed. Next in value were those covered with dense masses of grain, called "apiatæ," parsley wood. But the colour of the wood was also a great factor in the value, that of wine mixed with honey being most highly prized. The defect in that kind of table was called "lignum," which denoted a dull, log colour, with stains and flaws and an indistinctly patterned grain. Pliny says the barbarous tribes buried the wood in the ground when green, giving it first a coating of wax. When it came into the workmen's hands they put it for a certain number of days under a heap of corn, by which it lost weight. Sea water was supposed to harden it and act as a preservative, and after bathing it, it was carefully polished by rubbing by hand. The use of such valuable wood naturally led to the use of veneers, and the practice was universal in costly furniture. The word "xilotarsia" was used by the Romans to designate a kind of mosaic of wood used for furniture decoration. Its etymology suggests that the Greeks were then masters in the art. They divided works in tarsia into two classes—"sectile," in which fragments of wood or other material were inserted in a surface of wood, and "pictorial," in which the various pieces of wood covered the ground entirely. The slices of wood, "sectiles laminæ," were laid down with glue, as in modern work. Wild and cultivated olive, box, ebony (Corsican especially), ilex, and beech were used for veneering boxes, desks, and small work. Besides these the Romans used the citrus, Syrian terebinth, maple, palm (cut transversely), holly, root of the elder, and poplar; the centres of the trees being most prized for colour and markings. [See note giving extracts from Pliny.[1]]

A few notes on the exceptional scantlings of timber in antiquity may be interesting, though not strictly belonging to our subject. A stick of fir prepared to repair a bridge over the Naumachia in the time of Nero was left unused for some time to satisfy public curiosity. It measured 120 feet by 2 feet the entire length. The mast of the vessel which brought the large obelisk from Egypt, afterwards set up in the Circus Maximus, and now in front of S. John Lateran, was 100 feet by 1½ feet, and the tree out of which it was cut required four men, holding hands, to surround it. A stick of cedar, cut in

Cyprus and used as the mast of an undecireme, or 11 banked galley of Demetrius, took three men to span the tree out of which it was cut. It was the exceptional sizes of such pieces of timber, and veneers cut from them, which made the value of tables in Rome.

ITALY IN MEDIÆVAL AND RENAISSANCE TIMES

The mediæval craft seems, however, to have been derived from the East, though Theophilus mentions the Germans as clever practitioners in woodwork. A minnesinger's harp of the 14th century, figured by Hefner Alteneck, appears to bear out his remark, though later in date, with its powdering of geometrical inlays and curiously-designed sprigs, which might almost have been produced by the latest art craze, which apes archaic simplicity. It belonged to the knightly poet Oswald von Wolkenstein, who died in 1445; the colours used are two browns, black, white, and green. The oriental inlays of ivory upon wood, elaborate and beautiful geometrical designs, are still produced in India in much the same fashion as in the middle ages, for the possibilities of geometric design were exhausted by the Arabs in Egypt and the Moors in Spain; and in Venice there was a quarter inhabited by workmen of the latter race who made both metal work and objects in wood. Except for the inlaid ivory casket in the Capella Palatina, at Palermo, which seems to be a work of Norman times, we have no work of the kind which can be dated with precision before the appearance in the north of Italy of the similar "lavoro alla Certosa," or "tarsia alla Certosina"; but since inlaying with small pieces of marble and vitreous pastes was practised in central and southern Italy certainly from the 12th century, there is little difficulty in imagining how its use arose. This work has its derivative still existing in England in the so-called "Tonbridge ware," which is made by arranging rods of wood in a pattern and glueing them together, after which sections are sliced off—the same proceeding, in effect, as that which the Egyptians made use of with rods or threads of glass. One must allow, however, that the wooden border inlays, which are also placed under this heading, show greater craft mastery, as the examples appended show, which are typical instances. The chair-back from S. Ambrogio, Milan, is a characteristic example of the simpler form on a tolerably large scale.

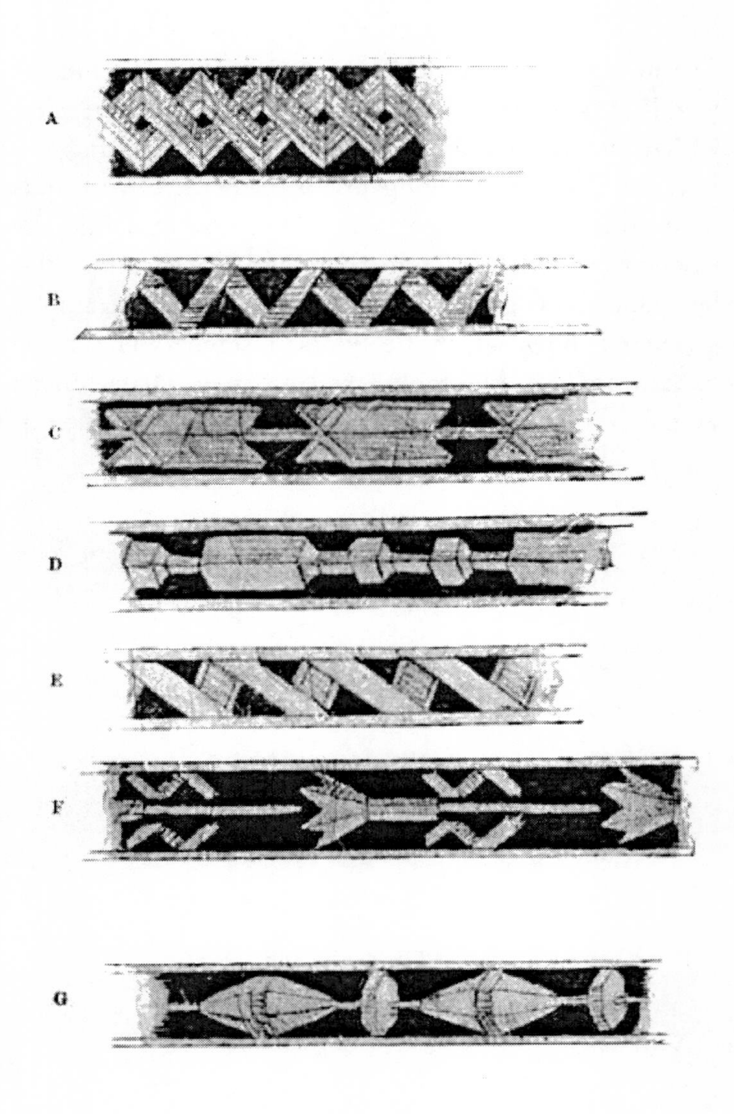

Plate 1.—*Patterns used in Borders*

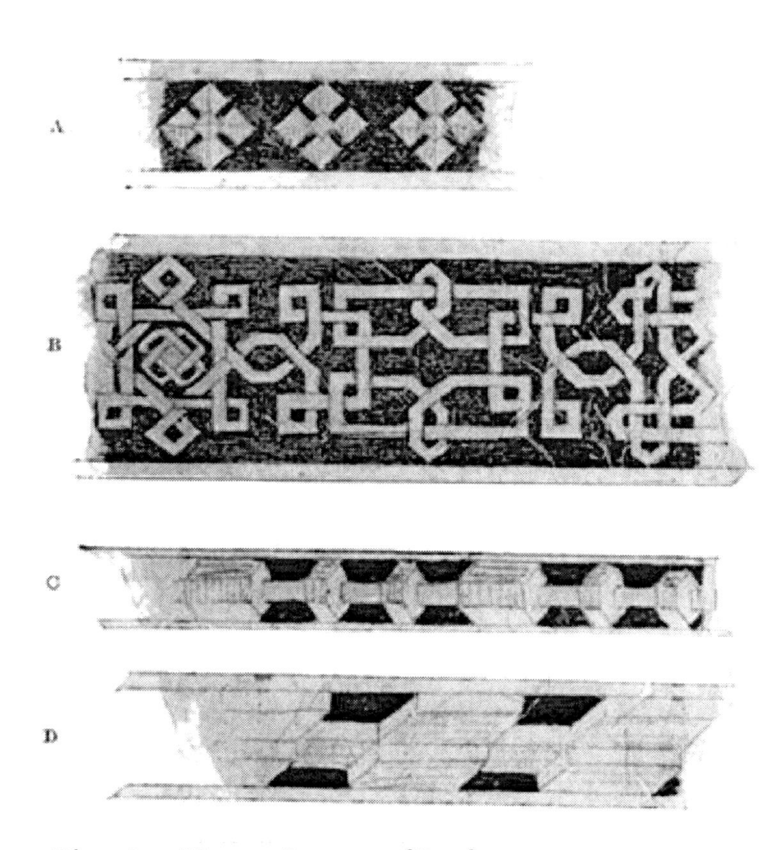

Plate 2.—*Various Patterns of Borders.*

Historians are agreed that the cradle of Italian carving and inlaying was Siena, where there is mention of a certain Manuello, who, with his son Parti, worked in the ancient choir of the Cathedral in 1259. Orvieto was another place where tarsia work was made at an early date, but the craftsmen were all Sienese. Mastro Vanni di Tura dell' Ammanato, the Sienese, made the design of the stalls for the Cathedral in 1331, and commenced the work, some remains of which are still preserved in the Museum of the Opera del Duomo. Twenty-eight artists were employed on these stalls; Giovanni Talini, Meo di Nuti, and others, all Sienese, assisted him, but he died before they were finished, and they remained incomplete till 1414, when Domenico di Nicolò is recorded as undertaking the work; but neither did he finish it, for in 1431 the overseers gave it to Pietro di Minella, and then to his brother Antonio, and to Giovanni di Lodovico di Magno. The woods used were ebony, box, walnut, and white poplar, and the cost was 3152 lire. In the 14th century tarsia was executed at Siena, Assisi, where in 1349 Nicolo di Nicoluccio and Tommaso di Ceccolo worked at the Cathedral stalls, which no longer remain; Verona, in the sacristy of S. Anastasia, in which city are some inlays resembling those at Orvieto, and Perugia, where some inlays remain in the Collegio della Mercanzia, but remains of the period are few, as may be expected.

Plate 3.—*Chair Back from S. Ambrogio, Milan.*

Domenico di Nicolò worked for 13 years at the chapel in the Palazzo Pubblico at Siena, using some of Taddeo Bartoli's designs, and also did the doors of the Sala di Balia, or of the Pope. This man, who was one of the best Sienese masters of intarsia and carving, and was head of the Opera del Duomo in 1400, and whose work brought him so much reputation that his family name of Spinelli was changed for himself and his descendants to Del Coro, or Dei Cori, is an example and a proof of the small profit which was to be made even then by conscientious and careful work. He was not only a worker in wood, in 1424 he also did the panels of the Cathedral floor, representing David and Goliath, the Amorite Kings, and Samson, ascribed by Vasari to Duccio; in 1415 he was paid 42 lire for a tabernacle made of gesso, while as early as February 28, 1397-8, he was paid 32 lire 10 soldi for 32½ days' work on a window above the pulpit; yet on May 13, 1421, he petitions the priors and captain of the people to this effect. He says that he is poor, and cannot meet the requirements of his family and apprentices, each of whom, he says, costs 30 or 40 florins a year, and therefore suggests that he should have two or three boys to teach, and that the priors should subsidize him for that purpose, and binds himself to teach them all he can without reserve. The priors and captains recommended to the council that he should be paid by the chamberlain of Bicherna 200 lire, free of tax, by the year, "nomine provisionis libr: ducentos den: nitidas de gabella," and should have two or three Sienese youths to teach, and the council passed the recommendation the same day. Twenty-six years later, January 14, 1446-7, he appears again in the records with a petition to the Signory. He says that he has always, from his youth up, done his best to provide for his family, and that by his craft he has always tried to bring honour on the city and spread the fame of his works. That as they know he was granted money to teach his art to any young man who wanted to learn it, but "because this art was, and is, little profitable, there was no one who wished to go on with it except Master Mactio di Bernacchino, who followed the art thoroughly, and became an excellent master." That, as he thought he was fairly prosperous, he gave up the grant (like an honest man!), but the expenses of marrying and dowering his daughters had been so great, and added to the losses caused by the small profits on his work, had reduced him to such poverty that he did not see how he could go on, being 84 years of age, or thereabouts, and having a sick wife. He therefore asked to have a small pension settled on him for the few years he and his wife had to live. He was granted two florins a month, but three years later all mention of him ceases.

Plate 4.—*Door of the Sala del Papa, Palazzo Comunale, Siena.*

The choir of the Chapel of the Palace had been given in 1414 to Simone d'Antonio and Antonio Paolo Martini, but they did not satisfy the public, so it was taken from them and given to Domenico di Nicolò, August 26, 1415. The tarsie are 21 in number, and represent the clauses of the apostles' creed and the symbols of the apostles. The unsuccessful work was given to the prior of the Servites. In the Communal records occur the following, March 31, 1428:—"Domenico di Nicolò, called Domenico del Coro, is to have 45 florins at 4 lire the florin for his salary and the workmanship of the door which he has made at the entrance of the Sala del Papa in the Communal Palace, which salary was declared by Guido of Turin and Daniello di Neri Martini, two of the three workmen upon the contract of the said door, at 180 lire. And is to have 3152 lire for his salary and workmanship of 21 seats made in the Palace of the Magnificent Signors, with all both '*fornamenti et facti*,' in full according to his contract"—accepted by Guido di Torino and Daniello di Neri Martini. He was called to Orvieto in 1416 to refix the roof of the Cathedral; he was not to have more than 200 florins a year, but if he came himself all expenses were to be paid. This suggests an appointment like that of a consulting engineer.

From Siena masters were continually sent to the other great towns to design and carry out works of architecture, sculpture, and woodwork, as entries in Sienese documents show. In early times the various arts connected with building were in close union, and it appears tolerably certain that one guild sheltered them all, proficiency being required in several crafts and mastery in one. We find the same man acting in one place as master builder or architect, and sometimes only giving advice, while elsewhere he is sculptor or woodworker. The painter, the mosaicist, and the designer for intarsia are confused in a similar manner. Borsieri calls Giovanni de' Grassi, the Milanese painter (known as Giovanni de Melano at first, a pupil of Giotto and Taddeo Gaddi; pictures of his are in the Academy, Florence, and in the cloister of S. Caterina Milan), "an excellent architect"; and he also worked in relief, besides conducting very important architectural works. He says that about 1385 Giovanni Galeazzo opened an academy of fine art in his palace, which was conducted by Giovanni de' Grassi and Michelino da Besozzo. On June 19, 1391, he was paid five florins for models executed by him, and something for the expense of execution in marble by another hand. In 1391 he was called upon by the Council of the Duomo, and after four months of uncertainty was assigned the position and pay of first engineer, with a servant who was paid by the Council. He did the door of the S. Sacristy; it was finished in July, 1395, when he was ordered to decorate it with gilding and blue. He also made designs for capitals and window traceries, and carved a God the Father for a centre boss of the vault of the N. Sacristy. He illuminated the initials, &c., of a copy of the Ambrosian ritual of Berold for the "Fabbriceria," and this was his last work, as he died July 5, 1398, and the price was paid to his son Solomon, the officials declaring that it was most moderate. His pupils were nearly all both painters and sculptors, and some of them became stained-glass painters. It is well known that Taddeo Gaddi was painter, architect, and mosaicist, and Giotto, painter, sculptor, and architect, and these details are an example of what was then continually going on. Both in mediæval times and at the beginning of the Renaissance the most celebrated architects often called themselves by the most humble titles—"Magister lignaminio," "maestro di legname," "faber lignarius," "carpentarius." Minerva, the worker, was the patron of all workmen from Pheidias to the lowest pottery thrower, and in Christian times the Quattro Coronati, the four workmen-saints, were the patrons of all who worked with their hands.

The oldest of the differentiated guilds appears to be that of the painters, at least in Siena, where one was established in 1355, while in Florence they were obliged to enrol themselves in the "Art" of the "medici e speziali," unless they preferred, as many of them did, to be reckoned with the goldsmiths. In Siena the Goldsmiths' Guild followed the Painters' Guild in 1361, while the workers in stone formed their guild still later. Among the painters were included designers of every sort—moulders, and workers in plaster, stucco, and papier maché, gold beaters, tin beaters, &c., and masters and apprentices in stained glass, also makers of playing cards—a most comprehensive guild. Vasari, in his life of Jacopo Casentino, architect and painter, says, however, "Towards 1349 the painters of the old Greek style, and those of the new, disciples of Cimabue, finding themselves in great number, united and formed at Florence a company under the name and protection of S. Luke the Evangelist"; and Baldinucci, in his "Notizie dei professori di disegno," prints the articles of association at length. Others hold that the Confraternità dei Pittori was not founded till 1386.

Plate 5.—*Figure intarsia from the Sacristy of the Cathedral, Florence.*
THE PROPHET AMOS.
This and the two succeeding are part of the same composition.

Plate 6.—*Figure intarsia from the Sacristy of the Cathedral, Florence.*
THE ANNUNCIATION.

Plate 7.—*Figure intarsia from the Sacristy of the Cathedral, Florence.*
THE PROPHET HOSEA.

The rapid rise of the last-named city in wealth and importance was the reason that so much of the best later 15th century inlaid work was done there, or at least by

Florentines, though the art was not new to Florence, the names of Matteo di Bernardino, Pietro Antonio, Giovanni del Mulinella, and Domenico Tassi being recorded as working there in the 14th century. Vasari, as usual, is somewhat inaccurate; he says that tarsia was first introduced in the time of Brunelleschi and Paolo Uccello, "that, namely, of conjoining woods, tinted of different colours, and representing with these buildings in perspective, foliage, and various fantasies of different kinds." Both he and Lanzi say that Brunelleschi gave lessons in perspective and "tarsia" to architects and others, of which Masaccio in painting and Benedetto da Majano in his inlaid works availed themselves. Vasari held but a poor opinion of tarsia, which, he said, "was practised chiefly by those persons who possessed more patience than skill in design," and goes on to say that the subjects most suitable to the process are "perspective representations of buildings full of windows and angular lines, to which force and relief are given by means of lights and shades"; that although he had seen some good representations of figures, fruit, and animals, "yet the work soon becomes dark, and is always in danger of perishing from the worms or by fires." He adds that it was first practised in black and white alone, but Fra Giovanni da Verona improved the art by staining the wood with various colours by means of liquors and tints boiled with penetrating oil in order to produce light and shadow with wood of various colours, making the lights with the whitest pieces of the spindle tree; to shade, some singed the wood by firing, others used oil of sulphur, or a solution of corrosive sublimate and arsenic. The "most solemn" masters of tarsia in Florence were the Majani, La Cecca, Il Francione, and the da San Gallo. The first name which he gives is that of Giuliano da Majano (1432-90), architect and sculptor, who executed as his first work the seats and presses of the sacristy of S. S. Annunziata at Florence, with Giusto and Minore, two masters in tarsia. He also did other things for S. Marco. In the archives of the Duomo, Giuliano di Nardo da Maiano is named in a contract for ornamental woodwork in the sacristy, to be finished in 1465. There is still existing in the Opera del Duomo a panel of S. Zenobio standing between two deacons, executed by him from cartoons by Maso Finiguerra, who designed five figures for the panels of the sacristy. The heads were painted by Alessio Baldovinetti. There are also several subjects in the sacristy, a Nativity, resembling Lippino Lippi's picture in the Accademia; a Presentation in the Temple, not without a reminiscence of Ghirlandajo's manner; and an Annunciation. The whole scheme of the decoration of this wall was Giuliano's, but it was the completion of work begun in 1439 by Angelo di Lazzero of Arezzo, Bernardo di Tommaso di Ghigo, Giovanni di Ser Giovanni detto Scheggione, painter and brother of Masaccio, and Antonio Manetti. Milanesi says his father was Leonardo d'Antonio da Majano, master of wood and stone work. He entered the Arte del legnajuolo in company with his younger brother Benedetto, and the first mention of his work in connection with the "Arte" is in 1455, when he made for the Compagnia di S. Agnese delle Laudi, which met in the Carmine, a chest with a bookcase of some sort. Five years later he carved some candlesticks for the Monastery of S. Monaca, and constructed some cupboards ornamented with inlaid work and perspectives for the Badia of Fiesole. Among his architectural work may be mentioned the Chapel of S. Fina at S. Gemignano, which Ghirlandajo embellished with frescoes. He commenced a choir for the Duomo at Perugia, decorated with both carving and tarsia, but since he went to Naples shortly after 1481, and died there in 1490, the greater part of the credit of this work must be given to Domenico del Tasso, who completed it in 1491. His brother Benedetto, to whom he turned over most of his commissions for tarsia, when he became much occupied with architectural work, was born in 1442. He assisted his brother in many of his works, such as the doors of the hall of audience in the Palazzo Vecchio, made between 1475 and 1480, representing Dante and Petrarch, with ornamental borders and other panels, in which Il Francione also had a hand. He gave up tarsia in disgust for the following reason, according to the story told by Vasari:—"He made two chests, with difficult and most splendid mastery, of wood mosaic, which he wished to show to Matthew Corvinus, then King of Hungary, who had many Florentines at his Court, and had summoned him with much favour; so he packed his chests up and sailed for Hungary, where, when he had made obeisance to the King, and had been kindly received, he brought forward the said cases and had them unpacked in his presence, who much wished to see them; but the damp of the water and the mouldiness of the sea had so softened the glue that when the parcels were opened almost all the pieces of the tarsia fell to the ground, at which every one may understand how astonished and speechless Benedetto was in the presence of so many lords. However, he put the work together again as he best might, and satisfied the King; still he was disgusted with that kind of work, not being able to forget the vexation which he had suffered, and gave it up, taking to carving instead." He finished his brother's presses in the sacristy of S. Maria dei Fiori, and, in the opinion of Vasari, surpassed him and became the best master of his period. He died in 1497. Vasari ascribes the celebrant's seat in Pisa Cathedral to Giuliano, together with another of spindlewood, "to be placed in the nave where the women sit," finished and sent home in 1477, and put up by Baccio Pontelli. Milanesi says, however, that the choir of this Cathedral was done by Francesco di Giovanni di Matteo da Firenze, called Il Francione. Guido da Seravallino, between 1490 and 1495, made for the choir of the sacristy of this Cathedral more than 15 perspectives; the usual price appears to have been 11 lire. He was a Pisan, and his father's name was Filippo. Domenico di Mariotto first appears in the accounts in 1489, when he began the choir and seats for the Campo Santo; he went on with various works of tarsia and carving till 1513. He was a Florentine, but lived in Pisa for many years, dying there in 1519. Other names which appear in the accounts are Giuliano di Salvatore and Michele Spagnuolo. In 1486 Cristophano d'Andrea da Lendinara and Jacopo da Villa came to make a seat for the choir, but this does not seem to have been a success, and Il Francione, who had been at Pisa as long before as 1462, and Baccio di Fino Pontelli, who appears in 1471, were put in charge of the work. Giovanni Battista Cervelliera is mentioned first in 1522. He was son of Pietro d'Altro Pietra, a native of Corsica, who began the singing gallery of the organ in S. Martino, Pietra Santa, finished by his son, who died in about 1570. In 1596 a great fire took place. After this the best pieces saved were used in the decoration of the new choir, in 1606, by Pietro Giolli, who also had some fresh ones made; others were mended by Girolamo Innocenti, and placed round the walls and round the nave piers in 1613. The pieces of Giuliano da Majano's work now remaining are in the side aisles, two at the right, one at the left; one represents King David with his harp and with a label in the other hand, "Laudate Pueri Dominum." The other two figures are prophets, and have scrolls, "Benedicam, benedicam," and "Ve qui condunt legem." Pontelli's Faith, Hope, and Charity are on the pier near the Chapel of S. Ranier, three half-length figures of women. The seated figures of the liberal arts on the side panelling of the church are Il Francione's, women with symbols, arithmetic, grammar, geometry, astrology, logic, and music. The great seat in the nave is the work of Giovanni Battista del Cervelliera. In the centre is a large round-headed panel with the Adoration of the Magi; at each side are three lower seats with architectural subjects in the centre and objects in the side panels and below the seats. It is signed and dated 1536. The whole collection of panels is well worth a stay at Pisa to see, even if there were not other attractions in that pleasant little town. In the registers of the "Opera" is an annual charge for two "sbirri," or two servants of the captain of the people, to watch the seats of the Cathedral "so that children may not damage them in the obscurity," which shows that even Italian children could not always be trusted not to be mischievous.

Plate 8.—*Figure intarsia from the Sacristy of the Cathedral, Florence.*
THE NATIVITY.

Plate 9.—*Figure intarsia from the Sacristy of the Cathedral, Florence.*
THE PRESENTATION IN THE TEMPLE.

Plate 10.—*Panel from Sacristy of S. Croce, Florence.*

Plate 11.—*Detail of frieze from the Sacristy of S. Croce, Florence.*

Plate 12.—*Lower Seats of Choir, Cathedral, Perugia.*

Plate 13.—*Upper Seats of Choir, Cathedral, Perugia.*

Plate 14.—*One panel from upper series, Cathedral, Perugia.*

Il Francione had a pupil called Il Cecca. His name was really Francesco d'Agnolo, but like most men at that time he went by a nick-name. Cecca is a corruption of

Francesco into Cecco, Cecca, from being Francione's companion and disciple. He was born in 1447; his father was Angelo di Giovanni, a mender of leather or "galigajo." He came to Florence from Tonda, a little place near S. Miniato al Tedesco. His father died in 1460; he and three older sisters were left to his mother, Monna Pasqua. So the 13 year-old boy went bravely to work to keep his mother and sisters, and entered Il Francione's workshop. When he was 25 he left him and set up for himself, taking a shop in the Borgo de' Greci, where he lived and slept as well as worked. In 1481 he had a commission from the magistrates, called "degli ufficiali di Palazzo," for all the wood-work of the Hall of the Seventy, Bernardo di Marco Renzi helping him. Afterwards he did other work for different parts of the Palace and for other places, all of which has perished. Finally, he spent most of his time as architect and engineer, and had a great deal to do with the fortification of various places and with the great cars for the "feste"—a not uncommon juxtaposition of engagements. He died in 1488.

The del Tasso lived in the village of S. Gervasio, and moved to a place near the walls of Florence, a few steps from the Porta a Pinti. Then they went into the city and had a house in the parish of S. Ambrogio, in which church Francesco di Domenico made a tomb for himself and his family in 1470. They had arms; at first they were a goldsmith's anvil (tasso or tassetto), and above a ball or heap of silver. Afterwards the field of the shield was divided, and they added in the upper part two little badgers (tassi) at the side of the anvil, and put below the keys of S. Peter, crossed, and interspersed with four roses. "And this they did, not only to point out the parish of S. Pier Maggiore in the gonfalon 'Chiavi' of the quarter of S. Giovanni, where the del Tasso lived, but also to differentiate their arms from those almost similar of another Florentine family of the same name." Evidently there was no College of Heralds in Florence in those days! The first of the family recorded is Chimenti di Francesco, who, in 1483-4 made a grating or gridiron of wood in the Chapel of S. Lorenzo in the Monastery of S. Ambrogio, and the dossal of the altar called "del Miracolo." In 1488 he carved a choir of walnut, outlined with tarsia, for the Chapel Minerbetti in S. Pancrazio, for which he was paid 100 florins of gold. He had, among others, two sons, Lionardo and Zanobi, who became sculptors under Benedetto da Majano and Andrea Sansovino. They also worked in S. Ambrogio, and the figure of S. Sebastian is by Lionardo. The two brothers in 1499 made nine antique heads of marble and bronze, which the republic sent as a gift to the Maréchal de Guise in France. Chimenti had two brothers, also carvers and joiners, Cervagio and Domenico, who brought up their sons to follow the same calling, who did many things for triumphal arches, cars, &c., for "feste." Domenico did the tarsia and rosettes in the seat backs of the refectory of S. Pietro, Perugia, and a credence of walnut, ordered on October 20, 1490, for the table of the priors, on which were festoons, griffins, and other inlaid work. The year after he finished the choir of the Cathedral left by Giuliano da Majano, and was paid

1404 florins, according to the estimate of Crispolto and Polimante, Perugian joiners. For the same choir he made the panelling of wood, for which he was paid 60 florins. There were 34 seats with ornaments at 36 florins each, and three with figures, which were estimated at 60 florins apiece. Payments were also made to him for work in the Sala del Cambio, sometimes for wood, sometimes on account of salary, so that it seems certain that he made the benches there on finishing the choir of the Cathedral, since they were being made between 1491 and 1494. The first cost 130 florins and 6 soldi in 1491, but it was not finished till the next year. Polimante da Nicola was made citizen of Perugia in 1473. Three years after he began the choir of S. Domenico, which cost 11 florins per seat. Four years later it was still unfinished. "Mastro Crespolto and Mastro Giovagne" were his assistants. Domenico had three sons, Chimenti, Francesco, and Marco, who followed the paternal calling. Chimenti was one of those who were judges in 1490 in the competition for the façade of S. Maria del Fiore, and in 1504 was one of those chosen to decide the position in the piazza to be occupied by Michael Angelo's David. Marco was an enthusiastic follower of Savonarola; in 1491 he was, with his brother Francesco, at Perugia helping his father, and six years later he undertook work there on his own account. They did half of the choir of La Badia in 1501-2, and the very elaborate lectern. The son of Mark was Giambattista, called Maestro Tasso, who was a fine carver in wood, and, in the opinion of Cellini, the best in his profession. He did many things both for ephemeral and lasting purposes, and became an architect, designing the door of the Church of S. Romolo and the Loggia of Mercato Nuovo, Florence, and superintending the construction of the latter between 1549 and 1551. In 1548 he designed an addition to the Palazzo Vecchio, then the ducal residence, and also under-*took to execute all the joinery. At the same time he made a model of the Palace which he intended to build in Pisa, which, however, was not carried out. He died in 1555. He was said by Vasari to spend his time in playing the wag, in enjoyment rather than work, and in criticising the works of others. But Cellini calls him pleasant and gay; Bronzino, good, lovable, and honest; and so does Luca Martini, who was a great friend of his. The following story of him, related by Il Lasca, shows that he was not above playing a practical joke of a rough character, and that he took great pride in the achievements of his fellow-artists:—"A Lombard Benedictine abbot on the way to Rome stayed in Florence, and wished one day to see the figures on the Medicean tombs in the sacristy of San Lorenzo carved by Michael Angelo, and having therefore gone thither with his two attendant monks, the prior of the church asked Tasso, who was then working at the floor of the library together with his son-in-law Crocini Antonio di Romolo, under the direction of Michael Angelo, to show the abbot the sacristy and the said library. Which abbot, after having seen the figures in the sacristy, and thought very little of them, set off to see the library, and while he was gently ascending a stair which conducted to it, talking with Tasso, happened to turn his eyes on the cupola of Brunellesco, and stopping to look at it commenced to say that, although it was considered by all the world as a marvel, he had heard a person worthy of credence say that the dome of Norcia was much more beautiful, and made with greater art. Which words so much exasperated Tasso that, pulling the abbot backwards with force, he made him tumble down the staircase, and he took care to let himself fall on him (!) and calling out that the frater was mad, he got two cords, with which he bound his arms, his legs, and all his person, so that he could not move, and then taking him, hanging over his shoulders, carried him to a room near, and, stretching him on the ground, left him there in the dark, locking the door and taking away the key." What happened to the unfortunate abbot after, and whether he was much damaged or not one does not know, for the anecdote stops here. Another instance of a family which devoted itself for many years to the production of tarsia and wood-work, displaying hereditary aptitude in the craft and gaining great repute, is given by the Canozii of Lendinara. The first member who took up tarsia, abandoning his craft of painting for that purpose, was Lorenzo Genesino da Lendinara, surnamed Canozio, to give him his full description. From him descended many excellent workers in wood. He studied in Padua, where he had Mantegna as fellow-student, and worked in company with his brother, his son, and a relation called Pier Antonio dell' Abate di Modena, who did the intarsia in the choir of S. Francesco at Treviso in 1486. He died in 1477, and is buried in the first cloister of S. Antonio at Padua, for which he made the stalls, as his epitaph states. They were commenced in 1462, were worked at continuously for three years, and after an interval finished in 1468. They were then coloured and gilded in places by "Maestro Ugozon de Padoa, depentor." Burnt in 1749, only two stalls remain, made into confessional boxes, in the Chapel of the Beato Belludi. The designs for the tarsia of the sacristy were made by Squarcione, master of Mantegna and Lorenzo, who was paid for them in 1462. There were 90 seats in this choir, so that it was a very important piece of work. A contemporary account by Matteo Colaccio (1486) shows what were the aims of the intarsiatori of the period as understood and admired by the more or less cultivated populace. "In past days in visiting those intarsiad figures, I was so much taken with the exquisiteness of the work that I could not withhold myself from praising the authors to heaven! And to commence with the objects that one sees around every day, here are books expressed in tarsia that seem real. Some are one on the other, and arranged carelessly, or by chance, some closed, some newly bound and difficult to close; candles of wax with the ends of wicks, now in well-turned wooden candlesticks, one straight, one crooked, less or more, with another crossing it. Elsewhere one sees clouds of smoke which spread out from new chimneys, fish which turn round from a full basket, a cithern which hangs from the centre of a narrow niche. Close by is a cage of bars expressed with wonderful spirit. Palaces, towers, and churches, through the half-closed doors of which one can see in the interior arches and windows, cupolas and steps. Most natural, then, is it not to be able to decide which tower to approach; these mountains appear to one covered with grass and with stones; and where earth of various colours appears there all green is taken away. But what shall I say of the images of the saints. Of their uncut and curled beards, of their hands, the joints of their fingers, their nails? Of their clothes, their sinuous folds, and the shadows? Nor less pleased me the little collar of rich pearls under the chin of S. Prosdocimus. Then round the angel Gabriel and the most pious mother one admires branches with such fruit and twigs that nature does not make them more true. And this is specially admirable, that through the dull colour of their leaves they seem to have been taken from the tree scarcely a day ago." And then he praises in a pompous fashion the folds of the Virgin's and the Angel's drapery, the silk veil over a chalice, and the perspective of a flight of steps which support the feet of the Madonna, &c. One of his first works was done for S. Mark's, Venice, in 1450. His reputation was much increased by the stalls of the Cathedral of Modena, made in 1472 by Lorenzo and Cristoforo, and restored in 1540 by Mastro Angelo de Piacenza, one of their pupils. He also worked at Parma in 1473. Fra Luca Pacioli (1509) makes an enthusiastic eulogium upon Lorenzo, "who, in the said art (perspective), was in his time supreme, as he showed in all his famous works, as in tarsia in the worthy choir of the Santo and its sacristy, and in Venice in the Cha Grande, as well as in painting in the same places and elsewhere. And at the present time his son, Giovan Marco, my dear comrade, who is worthy of his paternity, as his work at Rovigo shows, and that in the choir of our convent in Venice, and in Mirandola, the architecture of which fortress is well understood." In the sacristy of the Cathedral at Lucca are five panels from the seats which once surrounded it, signed "Cristopharus de Canociis de Lendinaria fecit opus, MCCCCLXXXVIII." One shows S. Martin, the bishop, full length, the others perspectives, perhaps of various streets of the city as then existing. He did these in conjunction with Matteo Civitale, and they were his last works. He died in 1491. Bernardino da Lendinara, who worked at Parma in 1494, and later, and was a citizen of that town and of Modena, was son of Cristoforo, who was also citizen of those cities from 1463.

Plate 15.—*Two panels from the Sala del Cambio, Perugia.*

Plate 16.—*Frieze from S. Mark's, Venice.*

Plate 17.—*Frieze from S. Mark's, Venice.*

Plate 18.—*Stalls from the Cathedral, Lucca.*

The stalls from the Cathedral at Lucca, which are illustrated, are now in the Picture Gallery. They were made by Leonardo Marti, of Lucca. When in 1620 the choir was spoilt (they thought that they were making grand improvements) they were moved to the church of the Riformati of S. Cerbone, being badly mutilated to adapt them to their new position. There, in two centuries of neglect they became in such a state that the brothers thought them no longer decent, and wished to sell them and make a new choir. The Opera of the Cathedral and the Commission of Art paid them something for them, and thus preserved them as they now are, having executed some restorations here and there.

At Ferrara are some remains of stalls in the apse of the Cathedral which were commissioned from Bernardino da Lendinara in 1501, though not made by him owing to the defalcations of a dishonest steward. In 1519 the Chapter of the Cathedral renewed the contract with Pietro de' Rizzardi and Bernardino, but as he died in 1520, M. Angelo Discaccia, of Cremona, son of M. Cristoforo (da Lendinara?), was substituted, and assisted Rizzardi till the work was finished in 1525. The gilding was done by Baldassare dalla Viola and Albertino dalla Mirandola. A note in the books of the Fabbrica, June 30, 1525, states that "Mro. Piero di Richardo dale Lanze" owes for work not yet completed 58 lire 20 soldi. There are three rows of seats, 132 in all, and the Episcopal throne in the middle. The upper row is of 56 seats, without the throne, the middle one 42, the lowest 34. Originally there were 150, but in the alterations of 1715 nine from each side were taken away, as the high altar was placed further within the apse. The upper stalls are divided by a chancelled column with Corinthian capital, and terminated in a shell hood. The intarsia on the back showed ornament of fine style, drawings of sacred objects and perspectives of fine buildings drawn from various parts of the city. Two of the best preserved show the ducal castle and the ancient ducal courtyard with the still-existing staircase constructed by Ercole I. in 1481. The usual bird in a cage appears, the symbol of human passions conquered by religious abnegation. The lower rows of seats are also worked in tarsia, but with ornaments of geometrical form, books, and joint-stools, the diamond, the cognisance of Ercole I. (who gave the original commission), and the pomegranate, that of Alfonso, and this last figure, which only occurs in the third stall to the right in the lower order, makes one think that only that part was finished under him. The frames surrounding are carved with restraint. The work cost altogether 2771 lire 8 soldi 2 denari besides the expense of making the lower seats, which cost 3984 lire marchesane 16 soldi 10 denari. The lira marchesana in 1523-25 corresponded to 43 Roman bajocchi 9 denari, about 2 francs 35 centimes of modern Italian money.

Plate 19.—*Lectern in Pinacoteca, Lucca.*

Plate 20.—*Two-leaved door in the Pinacoteca, Lucca.*

The Canozii were also at Reggio, in the Emilia, in 1474 and in 1485, but the work of the stalls in the Cathedral seems rather more archaic than their period, and the lectern is dated 1459. It is probably the work of Antonio da Melaria, who three years later made one exactly like it, with other things, for the Church of S. Domenico. This was done for Antonia di Fiordibelli, and the contract shows what were the conditions under which such work was done. He was given 50 lire at once to buy material with, 50 when he began working, 50 when he had finished a third of the work, 50 when it was half done, 50 more when three-quarters was finished, and the rest of the whole price of 336 lire when it was completed. He was to use wood of Piella, and give 48 planks to the lady—a very curious clause in the contract.

At Città di Castello there are tarsie designed by Raffaello da Colle in the Cathedral.

The choir stalls at the Certosa, Pavia, were made by Bartolommeo Poli, surnamed dalla Polla, from designs by Borgognone, as is said, and the style certainly seems to bear out the assertion, though no document has yet been found directly connecting him with them. They were restored in 1847 by Count Nava with wax and stucco coloured to imitate the missing pieces of wood. The upper row contains a series of figures of saints and prophets, and below are exceedingly graceful and flowing arabesques. A document in the Brera Library notes that in 1490 "Mro. Bartolommeo de Polli da Mantoa, who made the inlaid choir and the doors of the chapels, has a right to 8 ducats per door, and also for the wooden pulpits 30 ducats a pulpit." He was the son of Andrea da Mantova, who was born at Modena, but lived and worked at Mantua, and also with his brother Paolo in S. Mark's, Venice. The stalls were made between 1486 and 1501, and are the only work which he is recorded to have executed. A Cremonese, Pantaleone de' Marchi also worked on these stalls—a relation of the large family of the Marchi of Crema, perhaps, who worked in S. Petronio, Bologna, in 1495. The father was named Agostino, and he had six sons, Giacomo, Nicolo, Taddeo, Biagio, Agostino, and a second Giacomo. The stalls in the Chapel of S. Sebastian are signed Jacopo de Marchis. Some stalls by Pantaleone de' Marchi are in the Museum at Berlin, acquired in 1883. They probably came from Bramante's Church, the Madonna of Tirano, in the Valtelline, which was built in 1505, and where there are still some remains of seats similar in style. The upper range of panels has a few half-lengths of saints, landscapes, and the usual open cupboard doors revealing objects on the shelves within. On the backs of the seats below are arabesques, and the pilaster panels and divisions between are also inlaid, as is the cornice. He also worked at Savona.

Plate 21.—*Stalls at the Certosa, Pavia.*

Plate 22.—*Detail of Arabesques, lower seats, Certosa, Pavia.*

Plate 23.—
Panel from S. Petronio, Bologna.

One of the best Sienese masters has not yet been mentioned, Antonio Barili, much of whose work has perished, like that of many other intarsiatori, an example of which the collectors for the Austrian K.K. Museum at Vienna have picked up, however, where it may now be seen. He was born in Siena, August 12, 1453. His first work on his own account was the choir of the Chapel of S. Giovanni, in the Cathedral, Siena, of which a few poor remains have escaped the carelessness of the last century, and are in the Collegiate Church of S. Quirico in Osenna, 26 miles from Siena, on the old Roman road. The contract is dated January 16, 1483, and in it he engages to finish it in about two years. He was to be paid 50 florins of 4 lire beyond what he expended, and was to go on working at the rate of 10 florins a month. If he did not finish it in the given time he was to forfeit 100 florins, except for cause of infirmity, plague, &c. It was to be valued in the usual manner, and 100 florins was the penalty for the breaking of the contract on either side. As a matter of fact it took him nearly 20 years to complete. On one of the panels Barili made a portrait of himself at work, the one referred to above, now in the K.K. Austrian Museum at Vienna, which shows the very simple means used by the great intarsiatori. His tools consist of a folding pocket-knife, a square-handled gouge, and a short-bladed, long-handled knife, which he holds with the left hand and presses his shoulder against, so as to use the push of the shoulder in cutting, while in the right he holds a small pencil, with which he appears to direct the knife edge. The panel upon which he is at work bears the inscription, "Hoc ego Antonius Barilis opus cœlo non penicello excussi. Anno. D., 1502." He works in a window opening with panelled framing, and behind him a tree spreads across a courtyard against the sky, upon a branch of which a parrot is seated. Von Tschudi says that the panel is about 2 feet 10 inches long by 1 foot 9½ inches broad, and that the woods employed are pear and walnut, oak, maple, box, mahogany, palisander, and one as hard as birch in texture. A full description of it as it originally was is appended in a note taken from Della Valle's "Lettere Senese." It was valued by Fra Giovanni of Verona at 3990 lire. While this work was in progress he made the benches and other woodwork in the Cathedral Library for Francesco Piccolomini at a cost of 2000 lire, and did other work for private persons. Another great work was the choir of the Certosa of Maggiano, which has entirely disappeared. He was not only intarsiatore, but was much employed by the commune on architectural works. In 1484 he was sent to rebuild the bridge of Buonconvento, broken by a flood of the Ombrone, and in the same year, with Francesco di Giorgio, and on equal terms with him, restored the bridge of Macereto. In 1495 he was asked to make designs and models for a bastion to be erected over against the bridge of Valiano, taken by the Florentines. Owing to a bad guard being kept this was taken, and between 1498 and 1500 Barili was sent again to rebuild it larger and stronger. Finally, in 1503, he was sent to make designs and models of the new walls for the fortifications of Talamone, an important coast town. In his intarsias he was helped by his nephew, Giovanni, whose salary, when working for Leo X. at Rome, was five ducats a month. He died in 1516.[2]

Plate 24.—*Panel from S. Petronio, Bologna.*

Plate 25.—*Panel from S. Miniato, Florence.*

Plate 26.—*Panel from S. Maria Novella, Florence.*

Other names mentioned by Vasari are Baccio Albini and his pupil Girolamo della Cecca, *pipers to the signoria*, as good intarsiatori who worked also in ivory when Benedetto da Majano was yet a young man, and David of Pistoia and Geri of Arezzo, who decorated the choir and pulpit of S. Agostino in the latter town. Geri also made intarsie for S. Michele, Arezzo. Milanesi says Girolamo della Cecca was of Volterra, and calls Baccio, di Andrea Cellini; he was in Hungary in 1480 with his brother Francesco; they were brothers of Giovanni, who was father of Benvenuto and piper also. The stalls in S. Miniato, Florence, were made in 1466 by Francesco Manciatto and Domenico da Gajuolo; but perhaps the highest point reached by Florentine intarsia is shown by the stalls of S. Maria Novella, made by Baccio d'Agnolo from Filippino Lippi's designs. There are 40 stalls and 30 different ornamental fillings; the capitals, pilasters, and frieze are inlaid, the rest carved; the execution of figures, scrolls, leaves, and ornamental forms is as near perfection as may be.

Baccio, or Bartolommeo d'Agnolo Baglioni, was born May 19, 1462. "In his youth he did very fine intarsia in the choir of S. Maria Novella, in which are a very fine S. John Baptist and S. Laurence, and also carved the ornaments in the same place and the organ case"—so says Vasari. The organ case is no longer there, having been sold in England, but the stalls still remain. After carving the surroundings of the altar at S. S. Annunziata, which no longer exist, he went to Rome and studied architecture, of which Vasari remarks, "the science of which has not been exercised, for several years back, except by carvers and deceitful persons, who made profession of understanding perspective without knowing even the terminology and the first principles" (!) When he returned to Florence he made triumphal arches of carpentry for the entry of Leo X. But he still stuck to his shop, in which, especially in the winter, fine discourses and discussions on art matters were held, attended at different times by Raffaello, then quite young; by Andrea Sansovino, il Maiano, il Cronaca, Antonio and Giuliano San Gallo, il Granaccio, and sometimes, by chance, by Michel Agnolo, and many young men, both Florentines and strangers. He did a great deal of work for the great hall of the Palazzo Vecchio in conjunction with others, and the staircase of the Sala del Dugento. After this he did many architectural works, palaces and additions to churches, some of which are still existing. The design of Brunelleschi for the gallery to surround the dome of the Cathedral having been lost, Baccio was commissioned to make a fresh one, and a piece of it was put up; but when Michael Angelo came back from Rome he said it was not large enough in style for the dome; in fact, he called it a cage for grasshoppers (grilli), and made a design to replace it himself; as, however, the authorities could not make up their minds to accept it, and Baccio's work was much blamed, it went no farther, and was never finished. He died on May 6, 1543, at the age of 83, being still in full possession of his faculties, and leaving three sons, of whom the second, Giuliano, did a good deal of carving both in stone and wood, and architectural design, working in conjunction with Baccio Bandinelli, among which was the choir of the Cathedral of Florence. Another son, Domenico, showed great promise, but died young.

Plate 27.—*Panel from S. Maria Novella, Florence.*

The seats near the high altar at S. Maria Novella, and other things there were made between 1491 and 1496. The floor of the hall of the Great Council in the Palazzo Vecchio was begun in 1496, and with other works there went on till 1503. On October 1, 1502, he engaged to do the choir of S. Agostino Perugia from Perugino's designs at 1120 florins of 40 bolognini each, but he did not work at it much at that time, since on June 20, 1532, he made a fresh contract with the monks to continue and complete the choir of their church. Adamo Rossi gives other curious details about this work drawn from Perugian records, which are worth noting. He says that in 1501 Bacciolo d'Agnolo, not having a good design to show, agreed with the prior Federico di Giuliano in three months' time to submit two different seats for the choir of S. Agostino, and confessed to having received 50 broad ducats of gold as part of the price of the choir and the two stalls mentioned. He also agreed to return the money if he did not undertake the choir or did not finish it according to contract. He presented them accordingly, and in 1502 the contract was signed at 30 florins for each upper seat. Rossi also says that he finds trace of another Baccio d'Agnolo in the collection of wills of Pietro Paolo di Lodovico, under date June 11, 1529, and thinks that the work was done by him. One Baccio was elected capo-maestro of the Duomo in 1507 together with Giuliano and Antonio da San Gallo and il Cronaca (Simone del Pollajuolo), and continued in that office until 1529.

Rossi also gives other interesting details about the making of various pieces of joinery in Perugia and their makers, from which I extract the following:—"In the refectory of S. Agostino two Sienese, Giovanni and Cristoforo de'Minelli, worked in 1477. The cupboards in the sacristy of S. Pietro in Casinense were made by Giusto di Francesco of Incisa and Giovanni di Filippo da Fiesole in 1472. They were bought in Florence, and are particularly fine and large in their treatment of flowers, &c. The work was finished with the assistance of Mariotto di Mariotto of Pesaro, three workmen coming from places at considerable distances from each other, proving that they wandered about the country a good deal. The lectern in the same church, which is well inlaid and finely carved, was made by Battista the Bolognese, Ambrose the Frenchman, and Lorenzo. The contract was between the abbot and Fra Damiano's brother, Maestro Stefano di Antoniuolo de' Zambelli da Bergamo, and was for the whole choir at 30 scudi for each seat, wood being provided. The lectern itself cost 176 florins, and was finished in 1535. In the Sala del Cambio, besides Domenico del Tasso's seats, there is a fine door which was made by Antonio di Benciviene da Mercatello da Massa, for which he was paid 10 florins 93 soldi 6 denari. The orator's desk, the 'ringhiera,' was made by Antonio di Antonio Masi, the Fleming, though often ascribed to Mercatello. It was estimated by Eusebio del Bastone as worth 68 florins. At Assisi the choir of the upper church, which is the most important in all Italy for the number of its stalls, the mastery of its figure intarsia, and the elegance of its form, was made by

Domenico da S. Severino, who agreed with the superiors on July 8, 1491, to make it for 770 ducats of gold. It was not finished till 1501, but no payments are noted in the archives after November 18, 1498. In the lower church two Sienese worked in 1420, and a Florentine from 1448 to 1471. The choir of the Cathedral in the same city was made by Giovanni di Piergiacomo, also of S. Severino, and there is sometimes confusion between the two artists. The price was 57 florins. On one of the backs is carved the date 1520. The most ancient piece of joinery in Perugia is that executed for the Arte della Mercanzia in the 14th century."

Plate 28.—*Panel in Sacristy of S. Pietro in Casinense, Perugia.*

Rossi prints a priced list of joiners' tools, dated November 8, 1496, which is interesting as showing the small amount of tools and furniture required in a joiner and intarsiatore's workshop at that period. It runs thus:—

Bernardino di Lazzaro buys from Angelo di Maestro Jacopo, called Boldrino, joiner, the underwritten tools and apparatus at the price at which they were valued by Master Giovanni da Siena and Ercolano di Gabriele of Perugia.

	Florins.	Soldi.
Two benches,	2	0
Four planes,	1	0
Two screw profiles, one broad and one narrow,	0	40
Two rules,	0	16
Four straight edges, one large and three small,	0	28
One outliner for tarsia,	0	8
Rods for making cornices,	0	12
A cross beam,	0	6
Two compasses, one large and one small,	0	12
Two rulers,	0	5
Four one-handed little planes,	0	16
One two-handed little plane,	0	8
Two broad planes,	0	12
Two hollow moulding planes,	0	12
Three pieces of unfinished tarsia, and one with a wire drawing iron,	1	30
Two large squares and one "grafonetto" and one little square,	0	8

Two old irons for making cornices,	0	8
Nine files, large and small, round and straight,	0	30
Fifteen "gulfie," large and small,	0	24
Three chisels, one glued and one all of iron and one "a tiro colla manacha de legusa saietta,"	0	7
One small hammer,	0	16
Two arm chairs,	0	8
A big "tenevello,"	0	25
A little anvil,	0	20
A pair of big pincers,	0	32
Two little axes,	0	20
A two-handed axe,	0	25
A two-handed saw with a file,	0	60
A cutting saw,	0	25
Two stools,	0	16
Nine presses (clamps),	0	60
Two cupboards,	0	90
Five pieces of panels, two on the benches and three outside,	0	20
Three pieces of tarsia frieze and two pictures with a box without a lid,	1	0
A bench to put the tarsia on,	0	40

The words untranslated are, I suppose, Perugian words. At all events, they do not appear in the large Italian dictionary edited by Tommaseo and Bellini.

This Bernardino six years earlier worked as apprentice with Maestro Mattia da Reggio, and was paid 6 florins 22 soldi for four months. His name appears in the list of masters of stone and wood.

Plate 29.—*Panel from door of Sala del Cambio, Perugia.*

Frederic of Montefeltro, Duke of Urbino, built himself a splendid palace in that city between the years of 1468 and 1480, which cost 200,000 golden scudi. At that time a sack of corn cost rather less than five modern Italian lire in the duchy, and a hectolitre of wine only one franc sixty centimes, and one may gain some idea of the way in which princes of liberal tastes lavished their money over the production of works of art by comparing these figures. Among the decorations, which include much stone carving of the most extraordinary finish, which in the interior of the palace appears as fresh as the day it was completed, were some splendidly inlaid doors, eight or nine of which still remain. The palace was constructed upon the foundations of an older palace of 1350, much enlarged, and here he lived magnificently, and collected that fine library which was subsequently removed to Rome, of which Vespasiano da Bisticci, the Florentine bookseller, who had a good deal to do with it, says that it was the most perfect that he knew, for in others there were either gaps or duplicates, from which defects it was free. Castiglione's "Cortigiano," the ideal of a courtier in those days, describes the Court of Urbino as it was under Guidobaldo, his son and successor. Among the decorations of the palace which still remain is the panelling of a small studio on the *piano nobile*, close to the tiny chapel, which is entirely surrounded by intarsia of the finest description, which represents in the lower part a seat something like the misereres of choir stalls surrounding the apartment, some parts of which are raised and some lowered. In the spaces rest some portions of the duke's arms, a sword, a mace, &c.,

leaning in the corners, and on the lower parts of the seat are musical instruments, fruits and sweet-*meats in dishes, cushions, books, &c. The upper panels show cupboards with doors partly open, showing all sorts of things within in the usual fashion, and there are four figure panels inserted at intervals containing the portrait of the duke and the Christian virtues of Faith, Hope, and Charity which he strove to exemplify in his life. At one end of the room are two recesses divided by a projecting pier; in the one to the left the armour of the duke is represented as hanging piece by piece on the wall, in that on the right is shown his reading desk, made to turn on a pivot, with books upon it and around, and on the pier between, a landscape, seen through an arcade with a terrace in front, upon which are a squirrel and a basket of fruit. Close to the reading desk is a representation of an organ with a seat in front of it, upon which is a cushion covered with brocade or cut velvet, which is most realistic, and on the organ is the name Johan Castellano, which is supposed to be the name of the intarsiatore, though this name does not appear in the accounts. The custodian called him a Bergamase, I do not know on what authority. The designs of the figures are ascribed to Botticelli, and some of them look as if the ascription might possibly be correct. The only names of intarsiatori found in the ducal accounts are Beneivegni da Mercatello, who worked in the Sala del Cambio at Perugia, and no doubt had to do with the making of the doors, which resemble that work, and perhaps a Taddeo da Rovigno, the town from which the Olivetan Fra Sebastian came. Pungileone, however, found a payment of seven florins in 1473 to "Maestro Giacomo, from Florence, on account of intarsia for the audience hall." Dennistoun says that this study contained "arm-chairs encircling a table all mosaicked with tarsia, and carved by Maestro Giacomo of Florence," but it is now quite bare, though, fortunately, the tarsie are well preserved. He goes on to say that "on each compartment of the panelling was the portrait of some famous author and an appropriate distich," which leads one to suppose either that his information was inaccurate or that he was referring to the similar small study on the lower floor, in which Timoteto delle Vite did some painting.

The duke and his son Guidobaldo were both great builders, and Urbino was not the only town in which they raised palaces, though the others were not of so much importance. The names by which they were denominated show this. It is always the *corte* at Urbino, at Pesaro it is the *palazzo*, and at Gubbio the modest *casa*. Nevertheless, at this last place the intarsias were of almost as great importance, though now the palace is ruinous and the intarsias dispersed, some of them being at South Kensington. Dennistoun quotes descriptions from Sig. Luigi Bonfatti and Mr. F. C. Brooke, which are worth reproducing, as showing the care some times expended on the decoration of quite small apartments. This study, which was commissioned by Duke Guidobaldo, is only 13 by 6½ feet in plan, though it is 19 feet high. The inlaid work only went half-way up, as at Urbino, the upper part of the walls having been covered with tapestries. The tarsie showed "emblematic representations of music, literature, physical science, geography, and war; bookcases, or rather cupboards, with their contents, among which were a ship, a tambourine, military weapons, a cage with a parrot in it, and as if for the sake of variety only, a few volumes of books, over one of which, containing music, with the word 'Rosabella' inscribed on its pages, was suspended a crucifix. On the central case opposite the window, and occupying as it were the place of honour, was the garter, with its motto, 'Honi soit q. mal i pense,' a device which was sculptured on the exterior of the stone architrave of the door of this apartment. It appeared again in tarsia in the recess of the window, where might also be seen, within circles, 'G. Ubaldo Dx. and Fe Dux.' Amongst the devices was the crane standing on one leg, and holding, with the foot of the other, which is raised, the stone he is to drop as a signal of alarm to his companions. Among other feigned contents of a bookcase were an hour-glass, guitar, and pair of compasses; in another were seen a dagger, dried fruits in a small basket made of thin wood, and a tankard, while in a third was represented an open book surmounted with the name of Guidobaldo, who probably made the selection inscribed on the two pages of the volume, comprising verses 457-491 of the tenth Æneid." On the cornice was an inscription. It was thought to be the work of Antonio Mastei of Gubbio, a famous artist in wood, who executed the choir of S. Fortunato at Todi, and who is known to have been much in favour with Dukes Guidobaldo and Francesco Maria I., the latter of whom gave him an exemption from imposts.

In the 17th century tarsia was more used for domestic furniture than for stationary decoration. The character of the design changed in consequence, and mother-of-pearl, ivory, tortoiseshell, silver, and other materials were used. The first Tuscan, or one of the first who did so was Andrea Massari of Siena. A few works in tarsia were still executed, but none of much importance. The choir of S. Sigismondo, outside Cremona, commenced by Gabriel Capra and finished by his son Domenico in 1605, is one of the principal, and the choir of S. Francesco, Perugia, where Fortebraccio was buried, but this latter no longer exists. Marquetry was produced in Florence, Venice, Milan, and Genoa down to a still later date, but the fashion for ivory and ebony carried all before it. The Italian work of this kind is often most beautifully engraved, but less accurate than that produced in France. The later Italian marquetry does not lose decorative effect though the figure drawing becomes very conventional, and the curves of ornament are often cut with a mechanical sweep. A good deal of it is in only two colours, a return to the simplicity of earlier days.

THE CLOISTERED INTARSIATORI AND THEIR PUPILS

The Order of the Olivetans took its rise from the piety and liberality of a Sienese noble, Bernardo Tolomei, who, with two companions, Ambrogio Piccolomini and Patricio Patrizzi, established himself as a hermit on a barren point of land at Chiusuri, some miles from Siena, in the same manner as did S. Benedict at Subiaco. This was in 1312, but the Papal charter by which the Order was founded dates from 1319. It was called "Monte Oliveto," from a vision seen by Guido Tarlati, Bishop of Arezzo, the Papal commissary, in which the Virgin ordered that the monks should have a white habit, and that the badge of the Order should be three hills surmounted by a branch of olive. It was a branch of the Benedictines, and, like them, the monks devoted their lives to useful labours. As Michele Caffi says, "The Olivetans did not strive in political or party struggles, but spent their simple lives in works of charity and industry, and showing great talent for working in wood succeeded to the heirship of the art of tarsia in coloured woods, which they got from Tuscany."

The first master of intarsia mentioned among the Olivetan monks is a certain lay brother, "laico Olivetano," who came from Tuscany in the first half of the fifteenth century, and taught the art to the monks of S. Elena, the island which lies just beyond the Public Gardens at Venice, and was so beautiful before the iron foundry was established upon it. His principal pupil was Fra Sebastiano of Rovigno, known as the "Zoppo Schiavone," the lame Slavonian, who taught Fra Giovanni da Verona and Domenico Zambello of Bergamo, Fra Damiano. Fra Giovanni, again, was master to Vincenzo dalle Vacche and Raffaello da Brescia, and perhaps to the oblate of S. Elena, Antonio Preposito, in 1493.

Fra Sebastiano da Rovigno was probably born in 1420. The register of professions and deaths at Monte Oliveto Maggiore says—"In conventu Paduæ professus est sub die 15 Augusti, an 1461, fr: Sebastianus de Rovinio"; his death is shown by another extract—"Venetiis, obiit in Mon. S. Helenæ, anno Domini, 1505, fr: Sebastianus de Histria, conversus" (lay brother). He was at S. Maria in Organo, in 1464-5 and 1468-9, and at S. Elena in 1479-80-81, and again from 1484 to 1494. He was also at Monte Oliveto 1466-7, 1474-5, and 1482-3, and at S. Michele in Bosco, Bologna, from 1494 till shortly before his death, in all of which places were important works in tarsia. The inscription in the corner of the sacristy at S. Elena runs thus:—"Extremus hic mortalium operum fr: Sebastianus de Ruigno Montis Oliveti, qui III. id: Sept: diem obiit, 1505." Some of his work is in the stalls and sacristy cupboards of S. Marco, signed C.S.S., or S.S.C., that is, "Converso Sebastiano Schiavone," or "Seb: Sch: converso." His pupil Fra Giovanni da Verona was one of the most celebrated of the carvers and intarsiatori, and left works in many places in Italy. He was born in Verona in 1457, and no one has been able to discover either his family name nor who his father was. When still a boy he left his native town and went into Tuscany to Monte Oliveto di Chiusuri of Siena, the principal monastery of the Olivetan order. He may perhaps have gone with Liberale of Verona, who was of about the same age, the first time he went to Monte Oliveto, in 1467, or more probably on the second occasion, in 1474, his business being to illuminate the choir books. In the administration books of that convent it is recorded that in 1467 Liberale had as assistant a certain Bernardino, and in 1474 another whose name is not mentioned. This may have been Fra Giovanni, who might then have learnt to illuminate, which was his first profession, and in which he succeeded excellently. He resolved to "profess religion" about this time, and was received as novice in the beginning of 1475. The year of noviciate being passed he made his solemn profession on March 25, 1476, and remained for about four years more in the monastery, during which time he finished his studies and became priest. In 1480 he was sent for a short time to the monastery of S. Elena, near Venice. Here he found the lay brother Fra Sebastiano da Rovigno, whom he may perhaps have known before, since they were both at Monte Oliveto in 1475. At all events he spoke to him about learning his art, and finding him willing to teach him, "set about it with so much diligence and assiduity that he was soon able to give him valuable assistance." The work was on the cupboards of the sacristy and on the backs of the choir stalls, which were 34 in number. On these the principal cities of the world, as they then were, were drawn in perspective "with great beauty and cleverness." About 1485 he went to an abbey of Olivetan monks at Villanova, a small village in lower Lombardy, where he illuminated 20 choral books with heads of saints and prophets, with very beautiful borders of flowers, fruits, and animals. These were sold by an ignorant and greedy priest for 17 zecchins, and only a few of the miniatures have been recovered, which are now kept in the sacristy. Of them, Vincenzo Sabbia, the Olivetan abbot, who was "confratello di religione" and nearly contemporary, says, when describing the abbey and its treasures in 1594, that there are there "stupendous and wonderful choral books to the number of twenty, made about the year 1485, and rare and wonderful miniatures are among the letters, like lovely flowers in a delicious garden, and many most beautiful imaginings, heads of saints and of all the ancient prophets, and other wonderful things of like kind, made and illuminated by that celebrated Fra Giovanni da Verona, around the text."

Plate 30.—*Panel from lower row of Stalls, S. Maria in Organo, Verona.*

Plate 31.—*Panels from Monte Oliveto Maggiore, now in the Cathedral, Siena.*

In 1490 he was summoned to the Certosa at Pavia to estimate the value of the stalls made by Bartolommeo dei Polli, in company with Giacomo dei Crocefissi and Cristoforo de' Rocchi. Except for these there are no notices of the work which he must have done till 1502, when the abbot and monks of Monte Oliveto Maggiore, having determined to renew the choir of their church, confided the work to Fra Giovanni, and necessarily recalled him. He worked with so much enthusiasm that in three years he entirely completed them "to his great repute and with no less satisfaction to the monks." "The whole comprised 52 stalls, with their backs, seats and arm rests, kneelers and all things appertaining" (it now consists of 48 stalls and 47 pictures), and the panels of the backs were worked in tarsia with perspective views "beautiful to a marvel," where were figured houses, views of the country, cupboards, grilles, sacred utensils, and other fancies. In the early years of the 19th century 38 of these perspectives were moved to Siena and placed in the Cathedral, where they now are. Another choir, smaller but not less beautiful, was made for the church of the Olivetan monastery of S. Benedetto fuori della Porta at Tufi, near Siena. This church is in ruins; 31 perspectives from the choir were sent to fill the gaps in Monte Oliveto Maggiore, the monks who returned after the revocation of the suppression in 1813 having appealed to the Archbishop to allow them to take them. Four of the ancient backs were found in a corner of the sacristy, and eight carried to Siena and found superfluous were returned, as well as one which a neighbouring villager had taken. Some of them show the conventual buildings as they were at the beginning of the 16th century. The frames resemble friezes, and are decorated with flowers, fruit, birds, musical instruments, arms, and ornament. Each back is separated from the next by a colonnette carved with delicate arabesques. In this choir is also an Easter candlestick much like that at S. Maria in Organo, Verona, and there are two doors which belonged to the library. Pope Julius II. called him to Rome in 1571, and commissioned the ornamentation of the Camera della Segnatura in the Vatican, the designs for which are ascribed to Raffaelle, not only the seat backs with their seats, but also the doors, all worked with perspectives, "in which he succeeded so well that he gained great favour with the pontiff." Then he went to Naples and did the same sort of carving and intarsia in the sacristy of the choir of the chapel of Paolo Tolosa, in the church of Monte Oliveto in that city, works not less successful and lauded than those of Siena and Rome. This church is now called that of S. Anna dei Lombardi. The tarsie in the sacristy are in a later setting, and include nine panels of perspectives of landscapes, buildings, &c., nine others showing cupboards with objects on the shelves, and one with a figure of an abbot around which the following inscription runs:—

·T·EPRE·R·P·F·DOMI·DE·LEV·GNK·ABBATIS·ET R·P·ALOISII·DE·SALER·NO·PRIOR.

The work is exceedingly delicate, pieces of wood no thicker than a thick pencil line being often used. In one panel is a well-executed lily, in another a hare is a foreground figure, in another are an owl and a bullfinch, while a hoopoe appears in another, with mountains behind him. The objects on the shelves of the cupboards are turned at queer angles to show his skill in perspective, but, since they lack tone, do not appear quite accurate. Among the architectural subjects are the choir of a church, a harbour, and a castle on a hill, seen from a balustraded terrace, and a circular building a little like that in the background of Raffaelle's "Sposalizio." They were well restored in 1860 by C. G. Minchiotti. In the monks' choir in the church are other intarsie said to be by Angelo da Verona, Giovanni's brother. They are principally arabesques, somewhat resembling the panels in the Cathedral at Genoa, but include four figure panels of little angels and an Annunciation in two panels, which are not without charm, though rather overstiff.

Plate 32.—*Frieze from Monte Oliveto Maggiore.*

In his last years he returned to Verona, where he had made the monks' choir in S. Maria in Organo, and the cupboards of the sacristy. These have the reputation of being not only the finest of the period but also the best which came from his hand. The Adige was in this church for two months during one of the inundations, but the tarsie did not suffer so much as might have been expected. He accepted a commission in 1523 for some stalls for the Olivetan church at Lodi, S. Cristopher, eleven of which are now in the suburban church of S. Bernardino in that city, but died before they were completed. Vincenzo Sabbia writes of these:—"In the year 1523 the reverend father Fra Filippo Villani of Lodi, prior of the convent of S. Cristoforo in that city, agreed with Fra Giovanni Veronese, an excellent master of perspective, to make him 35 pictures of perspective at the rate of 30 or 40 broad ducats of gold for each—which are worth 5 lire 4 soldi each—which were to be finished in two or three years, and 300 broad ducats of gold were counted out to him. The said brother was not able to finish more than 23, because he died on February 10, 1525. They were sent from Verona and taken to Lodi, and in 1586 the new church of S. Cristoforo being finished, Don Agostino, the prior, who had charge of the fabric, had the aforesaid 23 pictures with their ornaments set in the choir by the hand of Paolo Sasono." He died in the 68th year of his age, and was buried in S. Maria in Organo. He is called "prior" in a chronicle of the monastery under date 1511, and in the list of dead. In his portrait in the sacristy, by Caroto, he is represented with the tonsure and with the hood and cowl of the form which was proper to monks who were constituted "in sacris."

Fra Raffaello da Brescia, whose name was Roberto Marone, was born in 1477. His father's name was Pietro Marone, and his mother was a Venetian, named Cecilia Tiepolo. When twenty-two years old he took the monastic habit as a lay brother in the convent of S. Nicolò di Rodengo, near Brescia, and a little later (in 1502) was sent to Monte Oliveto Maggiore. Fra Giovanni being then established there as "conventual brother," took young Marone and taught him, seeing that he had both liking and talent for the work, so that he soon became a clever workman. Between 1504 and 1507 he worked with him at the choir of Monte Oliveto, from 1506 to 1510 he was with him at Naples, when the famous sacristy panels were being executed, and in 1511 and 1512 he was at S. Nicolò di Rodengo, where he worked at the choir of that church. The lectern from Rodengo is now in the Galleria Tosi at Brescia; the inlays are in the lower portion, and show architectural compositions in perspective and the usual objects, such as a censer, an open book, &c. It is signed F.R.B. In 1513 Raffaello commenced the magnificent choir of S. Michaele in Bosco, Bologna, and here he also made the design for the campanile, which was built by Maestro Pedrino di Como, showing that like so many of the intarsiatori he was no mere worker in wood. While this work was in progress he executed a lectern for Monte Oliveto, ordered by the abbot Barnaba Cevenini, who was a Bolognese. It is signed and dated 1520, and shows on each side a choir book open, with notes of music and words. In one of the lower panels a black cat symbolises fidelity.

S. Michele in Bosco was among the largest of the Olivetan convents. The Benedictines entered into possession in 1364, but these buildings were destroyed by the Bolognese in 1430, "so that they might not give shelter and a base for hostilities to the soldiers of Martin V." The re-construction began in 1437. The choir was raised on several steps, and called "Il Paradiso," ten years later, but subsequent alterations have left very little of the original work visible. Raffaello's stalls were probably finished in 1521, that being the date on a panel which was formerly in the centre of the choir. Of these splendid works only two confessionals still remain in the church. At the time of the suppression of the convents at the end of the 18th century the populace, drunk with rapine and devastation, tore down these stalls, and they were sold for a few pence to the Bolognese marine store dealers and rag merchants. Only 18 of the principal row were saved from destruction, the Marquis Antonio Malvezzi buying them in 1812, and having them restored and placed in the chapel of his family in S. Petronio (now the chapel of the Holy Sacrament), where they now are. He was not able to save the hoods and shell canopies, which were sold for firewood for 4 baiocchi each! (about two pence.) The designs are of the usual style, cupboards and various objects in perspective; one of the finest is the first on the left, which includes a fine sphere and sundial, and several books written in German letters, black and red, a chalice in a cupboard, two books, and a cross. In the seventh is the figure of Pope Gregory in the act of blessing, and the last on the right shows loggias and porticoes of good style, well put in perspective. With part of the tarsie from

S. Michele pianoforte cases were made, other portions were used for the floor of the Casino, near the theatre of the Corso, and were worn to pieces by the feet of the dancers! In 1525 Fra Raffaello went to Rome, and no further notices of him or of his work occur till his death there in 1537; he was buried in S. Maria in Campo Santo.

Another somewhat similar set of stalls, though rather later in date, also at Bologna, are the upper row in the choir of S. Giovanni in Monte, which have on their backs intarsie representing monuments, fantastic battlemented buildings, musical instruments, and geometrical motives, all executed with a mastery which reveals an artist old at the work. They recall in their general effect those in S. Prospero at Reggio, in the Emilia, which were executed by the brothers Mantelli in 1546. They are set in a carved framing of arches divided by pilasters which terminate above in brackets which support the cornice. The pilasters rest on the arms which divide the seats. Champeaux says they were made by Paolo del Sacha.

The tarsie in S. Mark's, Venice, were worked by Fra Vincenzo da Verona, another Olivetan, under whom was Fra Pietro da Padova, Jesuit, with two youths to assist them. The commission was given in 1523. Three rooms in the hospital of "Messer Jesu Cristo" were assigned him as workshops, and 100 ducats for food and clothing, as stated in the registers of the procurators of S. Mark's. On January 15, 1524, they inspected the work done, and were not satisfied, and so suspended it, "praising, nevertheless, the manners and the life of Fra Vincenzo." According to Cicogna, the registers contained, under date April 7, 1526, a note of money paid to "Fra Vincenzio, of the order of the Jesuits, for the finishing of the works of inlay" in the choir of S. Marco. On February 25, 1537, certain moneys were given to more workmen for the construction of the doge's seat, which is said to have been "a great thing full of artistic pangs" (!), and rather hindered the genuflections to the altar. This was made for Andrea Gritti, who was doge that year. This Fra Vincenzo da Verona, or Vincenzo dalla Vacche, is mentioned by Morello in his "Notizie" as excellent, especially in his work at S. Benedetto Novello at Padua, four panels from which are now in the Louvre. He became novice in 1492, "Conventuale" of Monte Oliveto in 1498, was a priest like Fra Giovanni, and lived almost all his life in his native city. He died in 1531. The tarsie in the presbytery at S. Marco consist of seven great compartments, five lesser, and thirteen which are small. The eighteen smaller compartments are panels of ornament. The others are figure subjects, but by more than one hand. First comes a figure of S. Mark with a lion at his feet, which is not very good (it was restored in 1848-50 by Antonio Camusso); next, a figure of Charity side by side with one of Justice, a woman with a baby, and one holding the balances. Next comes a figure of Strength or Courage, older and rougher in character, then four ornamental panels, a door, and five others, also of ornament. The next panel in the corner bears date 1535, to which year the figures of Justice and Charity may be assigned. The other figures are Prudence and Temperance, the latter of which resembles Strength in character. The remaining subject, a Pietà, is like Charity and Justice, and is masterly. Three spaces are empty. The doge's seat, until the fall of the Republic, was on the right of the principal entrance to the choir, as Sansovino says. It had on its back a figure of Justice, now in the Museo Civico. He also says that Sebastiano Schiavone did these tarsie, but he died in 1505. Various initials appear here and there through the work; on each side of the figure of S. Mark are U.F.Q. and M.S.R. in cartouches, Charity and Justice have N. and P. at the sides, and Prudence has P.S.S. and S.S.C. attached to her. The panels of ornament seem to be of the same period as the figure of Charity.

Plate 33.—*Panel from S. Mark's, Venice.*

Fra Damiano of Bergamo, Fra Giovanni's fellow-pupil, attained, if possible, even greater reputation. He was considered the finest artist in tarsia of his time, he having, "with his woods, coloured to a marvel, raised the art to the rank of real painting." His family name was Zambello, he is thought to have been born about 1490, and he became a Dominican monk. An anonymous MS. of the 16th century, published by Morelli, calls him a pupil of a Slavonian, that is, Illyrian, brother of Venice, Fra Sebastiano da Rovigno. He passed the greater part of his life at Bologna, in the Dominican cloister there, into which he was admitted in 1528. In the records of the convent for that year occurs the note, "Frater Damianus de Bergomo, homo peritissimus, singularissimus, et unicus in l'arte della tarsia, conversus, receptatus fuit in filium conventus." At S. Domenico the choir stalls were his first work; he did seven, containing fourteen subjects and seven heads of saints. These were finished in 1530, and in consequence of their success he was commissioned to complete the choir. He carried the tinting of the wood farther than Fra Giovanni did, using solutions of sublimate of mercury, of arsenic, and what they called oil of sulphur. He is said to have had Vignola's designs for the architectural parts.

Charles the Fifth was in Bologna with Clement VII., and was crowned Emperor in S. Petronio on December 5, 1529. One day he was in S. Domenico admiring the works of art, and, doubting that the tarsie were made of tinted wood, as he was told, drew his rapier and cut a bit out of one of the panels, which has always remained in the state in which he left it in memory of his act. Desiring to see how the work was done he determined to visit Fra Damiano's studio. Accordingly, on March 7, 1530, he took with him Alfonso d'Este, Duke of Ferrara, and several princes of his escort, and went to the convent, when, being conducted to Fra Damiano's poor cell, he knocked at the door. The friar, having opened and allowed the Emperor to enter, shut it quickly. "Stay," said the Emperor, "that is the Duke of Ferrara, who follows me." "I know him," answered Fra Damiano, "and that is why I will never let him enter my cell." "And why?" said Charles V.; "have you anything of his doing to complain of then?" "Listen, your majesty," answered the lay brother. "I had to come from Bergamo to Bologna to undertake the work of this choir. I had with me these tools which you see, few in number, but necessary for the work in which it is my study to worthily spend my life, and to delight in the art. I had scarcely touched the frontiers of Ferrara when they not only obliged me, a poor friar, to pay a heavy and unjust tax, but the manner of doing it was most offensive. Now, while that duke allows such roguery in his State, it is right that he should not see this work which you see." Charles smiled, and promised to obtain from Duke Alfonso the amplest satisfaction. Going out of the cell he told the duke the reason of Fra Damiano's anger, and he not only promised to repay the loss which he had suffered, but conceded a patent to him, by which he and his pupils were for ever free from any tax or duty when crossing the duchy of Ferrara. Then they all came laughing and joking into the cell, and Fra Damiano, to show them that his tarsie were not painted with a brush took a little plane and passed it over a panel with some force, showing how the colours, after that treatment, still retained their integrity and beauty. And then he gave the

Emperor a most beautiful piece of the Crucifixion, and another to the Duke of Ferrara, who valued it greatly. Locatelli gives some conversations between Fra Damiano and his assistant Zanetto, which must have preceded this visit, which are worth recording for their racy expression, according well with his reported action. "If it were in my power I would nail up this door for Charles and for all the dukes of the world. This art which I exercise is exceeding dear to me, and I hate to have to do with these signori who manage things after their own fashion; and sad it is for those who have to endure it. I respect His Majesty the Emperor, and hold him to be a great man, but the fate of Rome sticks in my throat. That other, too, who accompanies him—" "Who?" interrupted Zanetto, "the Pope?" "Oh, rubbish; the Pope! The Duke of Ferrara. With him I have a special account, and he must not come here." He also adds the detail that Fra Damiano had no money with him, and had to go about begging for wherewithal to pay the duke's dues till he blushed.

From 1530 to 1534 he worked at a great piece of panelling to be placed in the chapel of the "arca," the tomb of S. Dominic, which is now in the sacristy, and thought by some to be his masterpiece. There are eight cupboards in this, and on each are eight subjects. In 1534 the Order was so poor that such expenses were stopped. Seven years later the work was recommenced and finished in 1550 by Fra Bernardino and Fra Antonio da Lunigiano a few months after Fra Damiano's death, which occurred on August 30, 1549. The choir consists of a double row of 28 stalls on each side, making 112 in all, showing on the right subjects from the New, and on the left from the Old Testament. Those on the right are the best, and are probably Fra Damiano's own work. He had as assistants at one time Zanetto da Bergamo, Francesco di Lorenzo Zambelli, and a lay brother, Fra Bernardino, who afterwards did the sacristy door. At another time his brother Stefano helped him, together with Zampiero da Padova, Fra Antonio Asinelis, the brothers Capo di Ferro of Lovere, Pietro di Maffeis, Giovanni and Alessandro Belli. The choir of S. Domenico cost 2809 scudi. Henry II. of France commissioned a little chapel from him with an altar-piece, for his reputation had crossed the Alps, and Cardinal Salviati and Paul III., the Farnese Pope, also wished for his work, as did the Benedictine monks of S. Pietro in Casinense, at Perugia. He did for them a two-leaved door, which cost 120 scudi, now placed at the back of the choir, and opening on to a balcony, from which one sees, in fine weather, as far as the Castle of Spoleto. There are four subjects, two on each leaf; the Annunciation illustrated is one of them. Sabba Castiglione uses the most enthusiastic language about him and his work. "But, above all, those who can obtain them decorate their mansions with the works, rather divine than human, of Fra Damiano, who excelled not only in perspectives, like those other worthy masters, but in landscapes, in backgrounds, and what is yet more, in figures; and who effected in wood as much as the great Apelles did with his pencil. I even think that the colours of these woods are more vivid, brilliant, and beautiful than those used by painters, so that these most excellent works may be considered as a new style of painting without colours, a thing much to be wondered at. And what adds to the marvel is, that though these works are executed with inlaid pieces the eye cannot even by the greatest exertion detect the joints." He then goes on in the same grandiloquent strain—"This good father in dyeing woods in any colour that you may wish, and in imitation of spotted and marbled stones, as he has been unique in our century, so I think that he will be without equal in the future; it is certain that our Lord God has lent him grace, as I believe, because he wished so much that things might be well ended, to put his final work on the work of S. Domenico of Bologna. I think, indeed I am certain, that it will be called the eighth wonder of the world; and as the Babylonians, the Assyrians, the Egyptians, and the Greeks boasted of their temples, pyramids, colossi, and sepulchres, thus happy Bologna will be able to glory in and to boast of the choir of S. Domenico. And because I do not wish that the love and affection that I bear to my most excellent father should make me to be considered a flatterer (!), a thing far from me, and especially with friends about whom I always speak the truth, I say no more; yet all that which I could say would be little enough on the merit of his rare and singular virtue, and on the goodness of his religious and holy life." Fra Leandro Alberti, in his description of Italy, speaks in something the same manner—"Frate Damiano, lay brother of the Order of Preachers, has become a man of as much genius as is to be found in the whole world at present, in putting together woods with so much art that they appear pictures made with a brush."

Plate 34.—*Panel from door in Choir of S. Pietro in Casinense, Perugia.*

A few stalls made by him are now in the church of S. Bartolommeo, Bergamo, which were brought from the Dominican church of S. Stefano, destroyed for the fortifications in 1561. The designs were made by Trozo da Monza, Bernardo da Trevi (? Treviglio), and Bramantino. As Locatelli says, they preceded the famous choir at Bologna, and show the master trying his wings. Some think that his best works are those in which he did not employ colour, but only shading, but general opinion considers his highest point was reached in the doors of S. Pietro in Casinense.

Another Dominican intarsiatore was Fra Antonio da Viterbo, who, in 1437, made the doors of S. Peter's at Rome by order of Eugenius IV., which were subsequently destroyed by Paul V. He was paid 800 ducats of gold before the Pope died, when they were nearly finished. They were both inlaid and carved in the most elaborate fashion, as the list of subjects shows:—The Saviour, the Blessed Virgin, SS. Peter and Paul, and Eugenius on his knees, the martyrdom of SS. Peter and Paul, S. Plautilla, who received the borrowed veil from S. Paul; the Coronation of the Emperor Sigismund in S. Peter's in 1433 by Eugenius, "and there you see the Prefect of Rome holding the sword before him, their march through Rome, the union of the Greek Church with the Latin, the entry of the ambassador from the King of Ethiopia, and other histories of the time." He had two assistants, Valentine and Leonardo.

Plate 35.—*Lunette from Stalls in Cathedral, Genoa.*

The choir stalls in the Cathedral at Genoa are attributed to Francesco Zambelli of Bergamo, a relative of Fra Damiano. He was helped by Anselmo de' Fornari, Andrea and Elia della Rocca, Giovanni Michele de Pantaleone, and Giovanni Piccardo, who had already worked in the choir of the Cathedral of Savona. The contract is still extant by which Francesco di Zambelli of Bergamo undertakes to make them with three of the procurators for the building and ornamentation of San Lorenzo, dated April 12, 1540. He agrees to get to work not later than the first of September next, and to stay in the city till the work is done. Nor must he undertake other work under a penalty of 100 scudi, which he is to pay in such case without demur or defence. The procurators agree to pay for every picture, with its frame, according to the design furnished to him, and they also promise to provide lodgings for himself and his family without any expense to him, and to give him a present when the work is finished. On the same day his relative, Fra Damiano, promises to make two pictures, one for the seat of the archbishop and one for the doge, to be ready by Christmas Day next, to be paid for at the rate of 27 scudi each, measure and design to be given by the signory. The same day the aforesaid "Magnifici" had it explained to them that they would have to pay the expenses of making sketches. In the panel with the history of Moses Zambelli signs his name and domicile. Fra Damiano's subjects appear to be the large ones in the panelling before the stalls commence, "The Massacre of the Innocents" and "The Martyrdom of S. Laurence." The figure subjects are not very successful, the arabesques are better; but the panels with open cupboard doors and objects within are not so well done as Fra Giovanni's. The stalls were restored in 1868, and a good deal of new work put in. The choir of the Cathedral of Savona was made in 1500 by Anselmo de' Fornari, a native of Castelnuovo da Scrivia; Pope Julius II. (della Rovere), who was born in the city, commissioned it. The intarsias are on the elbows of the stalls, half-figures of saints nearly life size, singly or in pairs, among which is a portrait of the donor, with perspectives of palaces, temples, or interiors on the backs. The lower stalls have less important subjects, such as censers, chalices, vases of flowers, animals, armillary spheres, musical instruments, etc. The cost of these stalls was 1132 scudi d'oro larghi (10 francs each and a little more) half of which was paid by Julius II. and half by the Commune of Savona. In the same Cathedral are a fine lectern, an episcopal throne, two doors of the chapel of our Lady of the Column, and a fine seat, the "banco dell' opera," commonly called "Massaria." Upon such a seat sat anciently the four citizens elected by the Commune to attend to the interests of the Church governed by them. Within this bench were preserved the diplomas, statutes, and arguments held to be most important to the greatness of the country. Anselmo de' Fornari was helped by Elia de' Rocchi, and the commission was given to them jointly on January 30, 1500, on which date Cardinal della Rovere promised to pay 570 ducats towards the expenses.

Plate 36.—*Panel from lower row of Stalls, Cathedral, Savona.*

Another intarsiatore who worked with Fra Damiano was Giovanni Francesco Capo di ferro of Lovere, on Lake Iseo. His masterpiece is the choir of S. Maria Maggiore, Bergamo. When it was determined to commence it in 1521 the presidents of the church fabric sent to various cities of Italy, especially to Milan, to consult over the model to be selected for so important a work with the excellent painter and architect M. Bernardo Zenale da Treviglio. In the archives of the Misericordia is a book entitled "Fabbrica Chori," in which is noted the great expense of the designs only, among which were some made by Lorenzo Lotto, by Alessandro Bonvicini, called Il Moretto; Andrea Previtali, Giacomo de' Scipioni, Filippo Zanchi, Giuseppe Belli, Domenico di Albano, Niccolino Cabrini, Pietro da Nembro, Francesco Boneri, and other painters, as well as the making of models and other similar operations. Those who worked at carving and tarsia under the direction of Giovanni Francesco were his son Zinino and Pietro his brother, who lived in Lodi; Paolo da Pesaro, and many others, including a whole family, Giovanni di Ponteranica and his four sons. The part towards the sacristy was designed by Lorenzo Lotto, the rest by Alessandro Belli. The sedilia on the Gospel side bear a signature hung from a tree, "Opus Jo: Franc: D. Cap. Ferr. Bergomi." The four panels outside the screen are Noah entering the ark, the passage of the Red Sea, the triumph of Judith by the death of Holofernes, and the victory of David over Goliath. Thus Tassi speaks of them—"These, to speak the truth, for their admirable workmanship, singular art, and beautiful colouring, do not appear to be pieces of wood put together, but rather pictures formed by an excellent brush, the pieces placed with such mastery, and the woods of different colours to form the chiaroscuro so arranged with the darkening of others that they make the half-tints appear as if really painted with oil by the same Lotto who made the coloured designs, and as he was a celebrated and finished painter and a powerful one, thus certainly these pieces of wood put together could stand in face of paintings by the most celebrated brushes, which, beyond the exactness of drawing, gave to their works singular force and finish; for in them all the possible excellences of drawing and of art are displayed, and whoever has had the opportunity of well considering them has remained surprised and delighted, never believing that human art could reach so high a pitch of perfection." His last work is mentioned in 1533, two pictures of Samson, at 60 lire each. In 1547 his son Zinino and his brother Giovanni Pietro went on with the choir, and finished it nine years later. The total cost for labour alone was 7000 lire Imperiali.

Plate 37.—*Panel from the Ducal Palace, Mantua.*

In Spain there must have been a good deal of intarsia done, seeing how long the Moors held the southern part of the country, but very little has come down to us. In the Mosque at Cordova was a finely inlaid mihrab of the 10th century, which was unfortunately destroyed in the 16th century and its material used to make an altar. In the Museum at South Kensington are some panels with Hispano-Moresque geometric inlays of bone of the 15th century, which are very pleasing; the ground is of chestnut, the bone is often stained green, and metal triangles and light wood are also used. This use of bone, which is frequently tinted, in conjunction with black and pale wood, is characteristic of Spanish work of the 16th century. The design is often exceedingly naive, employing birds, animals, plants, and trees, with scrolls and monsters. There is one cabinet at South Kensington with the animals entering the ark, which is most entertaining. The Portuguese carried this work on later, especially at Goa, in the 17th century, but neither here nor in Spain is the later work tasteful, except occasionally. Cabinets were then made at Toledo of ebony and ivory, and at Seville and Salamanca the same materials were used for chests and sideboards.

At Burgos is a pulpit decorated with inlay as well as carving, and one of the most elaborate works of marquetry of comparatively modern times is Spanish. This consists of the decoration of four small rooms in the Escurial, upon which 28,000,000 reals (£300,000) was spent in 1831. They are called "piezas de maderas finas," rooms of perfect or delicate woods, and are entirely covered with landscapes, still-life subjects, flowers, etc., made of the finest and most costly woods, and almost like paintings; floor, frieze, panels, window recesses, and doors.

There was a mode of decorating furniture much used in Spain and Portugal, especially the latter, in which metal plates, cut and pierced into elaborate and fanciful patterns, were fastened on to the surface of objects made of black wood by means of small pins. From this to the decoration of the same surfaces by sinking the metal in the wood is a short step, and some think that this was the origin of the metal inlay so well known a little later under the name of Boulle work.

Plate 38.—*Panel from the Rathaus, Breslau, 1563.*

Plate 39.—*Panel from Church of S. Mary Magdalene, Breslau.*

In Germany there can be little doubt that the art first struck root in the southern part of the country, the towns which produced the earliest furniture and other objects decorated in this manner being Augsburg and

Nuremberg. The first names of workers recorded, however, are those of the two brothers Elfen, monks of S. Michael at Hildesheim, who made altars, pulpits, mass-desks, and other church furniture for their monastery, ornamented with inlays, at the beginning of the 16th century, and Hans Stengel, of Nuremberg, but none of the inlaid work of either has come down to us. Two earlier pieces are figured by Hefner Alteneck, the harp already referred to on p. 8, and a folding seat of brown wood inlaid with ivory, stained yellow or light green, and black or dark brown wood, in oriental patterns, both of the latter part of the 14th or beginning of the 15th century. Two other names are mentioned as capable craftsmen in Nuremberg, Wolf Weiskopf and Sebald Beck; the latter died in 1546. The Augsburg work was much sought after, the "so-called mosaic work of coloured woods." The designs for the panels were generally made by painters, architectural and perspective subjects being most common, but flower pieces, views of towns, and historical compositions were also made. A German work thus characterises the later 16th century productions of this type—"A certain kind of intarsia becomes common in the German panelling and architectural woodwork; also in cabinets, vases, and arabesques, with tasteless ruins and architectural subjects with arabesque growths clinging all over them, of which examples may be seen in the museums at Vienna and Berlin, where one may also see works in ebony with engraved ivory inlays, which are generally more satisfactory. In German work, however, inlay was never of so much importance as carving, and the Baroque influence almost immediately affected the character of the design for the worse." At Dresden and Munich there were several celebrated inlayers in the 17th century, among whom may be named Hans Schieferstein, Hans Kellerthaler, of Dresden, and Simon Winkler, N. Fischer, and his son Johann Georg, of Munich, the last of whom, with his contemporary Adam Eck, practised relief intarsia, of which the latter is said to have been the inventor. It was known in the art trade as "Präger arbeit," which was not a name which accurately described its origin. Panellings of walls and doors were often decorated with inlays, most frequently of arabesques, of which the town halls of Lübeck and Danzig furnish fine examples. The "Kriegsstube" at Lübeck was done by Antonius Evers, who in 1598-9 was master of the joiners' guild, with his companions. The Rathsaal at Lüneburg was made in 1566-78, and the name of Albert von Soest is connected with it. Danzig, in the "Sommerrathstube," shows intarsias and decorations of 1596 in which the painter Vriedeman Vriese and a certain Simon Herle, probably a local man, collaborated. Other similar works may be seen at Brunswick and Breslau, at Ulm, in the Michel Hofkirche at Munich, and in the Cathedral at Mainz. At Coburg, in the so-called "Hornzimmer," are intarsias worked from the designs of Lucas Cranach and others, at Rothenburgh, at Geminden, at Landshut, and in many places in Tyrol and Steiermark, most of them much mixed with carving, too numerous to describe. The intarsias at the Hofkirche at Innsbruck, begun in 1560 by Conrad Gottlieb, may, however, be mentioned as being remarkably fine.

Schleswig Holstein is full of intarsias of the end of the 16th and beginning of the 17th century, of which perhaps the finest are in the chapel of the Castle of Gottorp. The princes' prayer chamber or pew is elaborately panelled, and the panels are all filled with inlays, mostly arabesques. The door and wall panels have elaborate architectural forms in relief with base, frieze, and pilasters; and are also fully inlaid with arabesques, counterchanged bay by bay. The ceiling is coffered, and the male and female patterns are counterchanged diagonally. Bosses of lions' heads and rosettes project from the surfaces of the beams, between which the intarsia panels are flat. The central features in the several divisions are sunk, a central oblong with an oval in centre bearing the subject of the Resurrection and two side diamonds. The panels surrounding these have raised mouldings, so that there is considerable variety of level, and the whole is raised on a bracketed cornice, the flat surface of which has small panels inlaid in the same fashion. It was put up in 1612 by Duke Johann Adolf of Schleswig Holstein and his wife, Augusta of Denmark.

Plate 40.—*Pilaster strip from the Magdalen Church, Breslau.*

In the State archives of Schleswig, in 1608, the names of Andreas Sallig, court joiner; Jochim Rosenfeldt, carver; and others are noted. Also in 1609, with the addition of the painter Herman Uhr and Hans and Jürgen Dreyer, of Schleswig; also the carver Hans Preuszen, and Adam Wegener, the figure-cutter. In 1610 the names of Jürgen Koningh, joiner's workman, several carvers, and Herman Uhr, the painter, occur. In 1611 Herman Uhr and Klaus Barck work in the chapel, the first for 115 days, and the second for 178 days, and in 1612 several carvers and turners work for a long time at the rate of five "schillings" a day, as well as Herman Uhr and his assistant. These records distinctly suggest that the painter Herman Uhr was the designer, since his name is the only one which appears for four years consecutively, though the long period during which he worked in 1612 may be explained by the number of paintings which cover a portion of the exterior of the pew.

Plate 41.—*Panel from S. Elizabeth's Church, Breslau.*

In South Germany one often meets with musical instruments which are inlaid with conventionalised floral forms. They were produced in the 17th century in considerable quantities in Wurtemburg, Bavaria, and on the Southern Shores of Lake Constance. Nor must one forget the extraordinarily elaborate ivory inlays on the stocks of arquebuses. In the Wallace collection are many examples, and attention may be drawn to a jewel box made in 1630 by Conrad Cornier, arquebus mounter, which is decorated with most elaborate scrolls, leaves, and birds of ivory and mother-of-pearl, stained green in parts. It is made of walnut, and has metal scrolls at the corners of the panel framing. The German inlays on the whole rather run to arabesques and strapwork, or naturalistic vases of flowers, with butterflies and birds; one meets occasional perspectives and even figures, but the work is generally harder and less successful than the Italian technique, with a larger and less intelligent use of scorched tints.

In the latter part of the 17th century they often made the ground of a cabinet or panelling of one wood and the mouldings which defined the panels and the carved ornaments added of another, or even of two others; the effect is not quite happy. Tortoiseshell also appears, and metal and coloured stones; the striving after what they thought to be greater artistry soon caused them to outstep more and more the proper limits of the art, and brought about decadence. The South German bride chests of the century before are decorated a good deal with inlays, Peter Flotner's designs often serving as patterns; a little green and red appear mixed with the commoner colours. The architectural forms project, and would form a tolerable design by themselves, though scarcely suitable to the object to which they are applied. In German work the cabinets are often of the most elaborate architectural design, like the façade of a palace, made of ebony, or occasionally even of ivory, and inlaid with ivory, silver, gold and enamels or precious stones. Augsburg was the most celebrated place for such work. The joiner, the woodcarver, the lapidary, and the goldsmith all worked together on such things. In the North of Germany tarsia was principally used on chests, cabinets, seats, and smaller objects of furniture; in South Germany, where the Italian influence was stronger, it was much used in wall-panelling and the panels of doors. The little castle of Völthurn, near Brixen, built by the bishop of that town in 1580-85 and decorated by Brixener artists and joiners (now belonging to Prince Lichtenstein), shows "panelled walls with architectural features, columns, cornices, and friezes, with gabled doorways with columns and pediments, decorated with very delicate intarsias, foliage ornaments, flowers, and fruit, a work which modern Brixener joiners could with difficulty understand"; so says Von Falke. Ebony and ivory work came to Germany in the latter half of the 16th century, when Augsburg and Nuremberg soon exported their productions of this sort to all the world, and with this commercial production the use of male and female designs begins, black on white and white on black. The latter is the better and more valued. Hans Schieferstein's cabinet, now at Dresden, a work of this period, has an ingenious use of this mode of inlay. It is made of ebony or veneered with that wood, and has inlays of brown cypress and of ivory. The panel on the inside of the door is of the same design as that on the outside, but what was white becomes brown, what was brown is black, and the black becomes white.

Plate 42.—*Lower panel of door, 1564—Tyrolese.*

In the Musée Cluny is a wire drawing bench made in 1565 for Augustus I., Elector of Saxony, who was an amateur craftsman. The two longitudinal surfaces are covered with a double frieze of marquetry, one side representing a satirical tournament between the Papacy and Lutheranism, and the other a carousal of wild men. In front one sees the marqueteur with his tools doing his work, below which he has placed his monogram, L—D., accompanied by a cup.

In the Museum at Leipzig is a very fine cabinet, with many drawers within, elaborately inlaid with arabesques on a light ground, with a few architectural forms in ebony projecting. It is Tyrolese work of the beginning of the 17th century, and is a typical example. To the few names of German intarsiatori may be added those of Isaac Kiening, of Frissen, and Sixtus Loblein, of Landshut.

In the lower Rhine and in Holland tarsia was used for great and small chests, sideboards and doors with rich gable crownings, with good drawing of flowers, and sprigs of leaves with birds and beasts among them, the ground being generally light. The doors ordered by the Swedish Chamberlain, Axel Oxenstiern, now in the drinking-room of the King's Castle of Ulriksdal, near Stockholm, are said by Von Falke to be the finest examples extant of this kind of work, and to have been made in the 17th century by a Dutch craftsman. The best period in Holland was the second half of the 16th and the first half of the 17th century. In the work of this period the handling is broad, and the composition often a little over-full, but the many different woods which

Dutch commerce made available seduced the marqueteurs into too pictorial a treatment in point of colour. Their reputation was so great that Colbert engaged two Dutch marqueteurs, Pierre Gole and Vordt, for the Gobelins at the beginning of the 17th century, and Jean Macé also learnt the craft by a long stay in Holland. Here, as well as in France and Italy, rich chairs were commonly decorated with marquetry, and in William and Mary's reign such things became the fashion in England. The design employed tulips and other flowers, foliage, birds, etc., all in gay colours; ivory and mother-of-pearl were used occasionally for salient points, such as eyes. Examples of the use and misuse of these materials may be seen in the Victoria and Albert Museum at South Kensington.

Plate 43.—*Top of card table in the Drawing-room, Roehampton House. Dutch, 18th Century.*

Plate 44.—*Panelling from Sizergh Castle, now in Victoria and Albert Museum.*

Although not much work of importance is known in England which is certainly the production of native craftsmen, a few notable examples may be called to mind, such as the room from Sizergh Castle, now at South Kensington, with inlays of holly and bog-oak, and the fine suite of furniture at Hardwick Hall, made for Bess of Hardwick by English workmen who had been to Italy for some years. Correspondence passed between her and Sir John Thynne on the subject of the craftsmen employed by both, and there seems no doubt that Longleat and Hardwick were the work of the same men. The inlays upon the long table are particularly fine, and except for a certain clumsiness almost recall the glories of the great period of Italian marquetry. The cradle of James I. (1566) is enriched with inlays.

At Gilling Castle, near Wakefield, are some panels inlaid with flowers, etc., which local tradition says were executed by some of the ladies of the family, which probably points to their having been done under their superintendence by local workmen, and small panels of rough inlay are not uncommon in chest and bedstead, overmantel and cabinet from the Jacobean period onward. S. Mary Overie, Southwark, possesses a fine parish chest decorated with a good deal of Dutch-looking inlay in conjunction with carving, and a rather unusual piece of work may be seen at Glastonbury Hall, where the treads and landings of the oak stairs are inlaid with mahogany and a light wood with stars and lozenges and a cartouche with a monogram and date 1726. The use of satin wood came into fashion towards the end of the eighteenth century, and was accompanied by a delicate inlay of other woods, which, however, scarcely went beyond the simplest ornament, since the decoration of furniture by means of painting became fashionable at nearly the same period.

Plate 45.—*Cabinet with falling front, in the drawing-room, Roehampton House.*

It was in France that the most wonderful achievements of the later marqueteurs were produced, which have made French furniture recognised by the public as well as by connoisseurs as an art manufacture, in conjunction with the wonderfully chiselled ormolu mountings. Mention is made of intarsia in France as early as the end of the fifteenth century, however. In the inventory of Anne of Brittanny's effects (1498) may be read "ung coffret faict de musayeque de bois et d'ivoire," and in a still earlier one of the Duke de Berry's, dated 1416, is mentioned a "grant tableau, où est la passion de Nostre Seigneur, fait de poins de marqueterie." This is as early as the intarsias of Domenico di Nicolò at Siena, and was probably of foreign manufacture. In 1576 a certain Hans Kraus was called "marqueteur du roi," but the first Frenchman known to have practised the art is Jean Macé of Blois, who was at work in Paris from 1644 or earlier to 1672 as sculptor and painter. He is said to have been the first who brought intarsia into France, under the name of "marqueterie," having been for some time in the Netherlands. His title was "menuisier et faiseur de Cabinets et tableaux en marqueterie de bois." He was lodged in the Louvre in 1644 (when Louis XIV. was six years old), "en honneur de la longue et belle pratique de son art dans les Pays Bas." His daughter married Pierre Boulle, who in 1619 was turner and joiner to the King, probably both to Louis XIII. and Henry IV. In 1621 Paul Boulle was born, and five years later Jacques. The family was settled at Charenton-le-Pont, near Paris, the principal town of the Huguenots for eighty years. Here, in 1649, Pierre Boulle was buried, the father of seven children. The earlier seventeenth century designs show picturesque landscapes or broken ruins or figures, *motifs* which recur a century later, as in the beautiful panel signed "Follet" in the Cabinet by Claude Charles Saunier in the Wallace collection. The colours are occasionally stained, and ebony and ivory are favourite materials. It is impossible to fix the exact time when copper and tortoiseshell came into use in France. Some of the cabinets in which they appear are certainly of the period of Louis XIII. It was probably imported either from Spain or Flanders; it became very fashionable about the middle of the seventeenth century, and ended by entirely absorbing the official orders of the Court of Louis XIV. With this work the name of Boulle is indissolubly associated. Pierre Boulle was lodged in the Louvre about 1642. In 1636 he is on the list for 400 livres annually. Jean Boulle died in the Louvre in 1680. He was the father of André Charles probably, who was born in November, 1642, and the nephew of Pierre. André Charles Boulle in 1672 succeeded to the lodging of Jean Macé in the same building, and seven years later by a second brévet to the "demilogement," formerly occupied by Guillaume Petit "to allow him to finish the works executed for His Majesty's service." It is told of him by a contemporary that the talented boy wanted to be a painter, but his father would not allow it, and insisted upon his keeping to handicraft. He was a man of most varied talent; when he was first granted apartments in the Louvre it was as "joiner, marqueteur, gilder, and chiseller," and in the decree of Louis XIV., by which he was appointed the first art-joiner to the King, he is called "architect, sculptor, and engraver." He had a passion for collecting drawings, paintings, and other works of art, and when his workshops were burnt his collection was valued at 60,000 livres. This taste brought him into money difficulties, and in 1704 his creditors obtained a decree against him, and he would have been imprisoned if the King had not extended the safeguard of the Palace of the Louvre to him on condition that he made an arrangement with them. He was a member of the Academy of S. Luke as sculptor and brass engraver. The Cabinet of the Dauphin was considered his masterpiece, in which the walls and ceiling were covered with mirrors in ebony frames, with inlays of rich gilding, and the floor laid with wood mosaic, in which the initials of the Dauphin and his wife were intertwined. The drawing made for it is now in the Musée des Arts Décoratifs, but the work itself no longer exists. On August 30th, 1720, his works were burnt, it was thought by a thief whom the workmen of Marteau, his neighbour at the Louvre, had surprised some months before and punished summarily, who, by way of vengeance on the "menuisiers," set fire to the "ébénistes." Nearly everything he possessed was either burnt, lost, or stolen; models of the value of 37,000 livres, wood and tools worth 25,000, many pieces of furniture finished or in course of construction; works in metal, as well as in wood, and his whole collection of drawings, paintings, and objects of art. His total loss was estimated by experts at 383,780 livres, more than 1,000,000 of francs in the money of to-day, from which an income of 50,000 francs might be expected. This valuation was on an inventory drawn up shortly after, perhaps for the purpose of getting the King's help. The number of undeniable productions of his hand is small, but objects which came from the studio after his death are tolerably plentiful since his four sons carried on the business, though not the inspiration; contemporaries characterised them as "apes." Two commodes which were in Louis XVI.'s bedroom at Versailles are now in the Bibliothêque Mazarin, and a chest which was forgotten in the Custom House at Havre now belongs to the museum of that city. A cabinet is in the Mobilier National, and a pedestal is in the Grünes Gewölbe at Dresden. Other genuine Boulles are in the Wallace collection, in the Rothschild collection, and at the Hotel Cluny. A writing table, for which the millionaire Samuel Bernard (who died in 1739), a great collector of art treasures, had given 50,000 livres, appears to be lost. M. Luchet asks, with some truth, "Can you imagine a financier, Jew or Christian, paying 100,000 francs for a new bureau? Old, it would be another thing—an object of art to sell." Boulle was most careful over his materials. He had 12,000 livres worth of wood in his stores, fir, oak, walnut, battens, Norwegian wood, all collected and kept long and carefully for the benefit of the work. He also used real tortoiseshell, which, is replaced in the economical art industry of the day with gelatine. The mountings were always chiselled, cast quite roughly, so that the artist did nearly everything. He was helped in this part of the work by Domenico Cucci and others. The inlay, instead of being tortoiseshell, may have been horn, mother-of-pearl, ivory, or wood; the motive, instead of brass, may be pewter, silver, aluminium, or gold; it is still known by the name of Boulle work. Boulle himself worked intarsia of wood also at intervals all through his life. He died February 29th, 1732.

Plate 46.—*Cabinet belonging to Earl Granville. Boulle work of about 1740.*

Plate 47.—*Top of writing table in the Saloon, Roehampton House. Period of Louis XV.*

Plate 48.—*Encoignure, signed J. F. Oeben, in the Jones bequest, Victoria and Albert Museum.*

His pupil, J. F. Oëben, became "ébéniste du roi," with a lodging in the *dépendances* of the Arsenal in 1754. He was marqueteur especially. Examples of his work are both at South Kensington and in the Wallace collection, and in the Gallerie d'Apollon at the Louvre is the great secretary bureau, which he was making for Louis XV. at the time of his death, in or about 1765. His widow carried on the establishment; her foreman, J. Henry Riesener, completed the unfinished work. He was also a German, born in 1735 at Gladbach, near Cologne, and coming to Paris quite young entered Oëben's atelier. On his death he was made foreman, and two years after, when he was thirty-two years of age, married his master's widow. The year following 1768 he was received as master *menuisier ébéniste*. In 1776 his wife died, and six years after he married again, but was divorced as soon as the new legislation allowed it. When he was married the first time he had no fortune, but fifteen years after he declared in his marriage contract that there was then owing to him by the King, the royal family, and other debtors 504,571 livres, without counting the finished objects in his warehouses, his models of bronze, his jewels, and personal effects, and several important life annuities. Between 1775 and 1785 he received from the Garde Meuble 500,000 livres, so profitable had the production of furniture of the highest class become. He was in full work at the time of the Revolution, and two of his finest pieces bear the dates 1790 and 1791 in their marquetry. When the furniture of the royal residences was sold, Riesener bought back several pieces, being aided by Charles Delacroix, the husband of his first wife's daughter, who directed the sale at Versailles. He tried to sell these again, but with poor success, and when he died, on January 8th, 1806, at the age of 71, he was again almost without fortune. His beautiful bureau secretary in the Wallace collection, made for Stanislas Leczinski, King of Poland, and dated 1769, shows him at his best. The workmanship is superb, and the design most pleasing, almost the only point to which exception may be taken being the crude green, obtained by staining, here and there. The half-length of Secrecy in the oval cartouche at the back is as good as the best Italian figure work, and was often reproduced by him. The flower panels are particularly delicate and beautiful. There is an upright secretary, also by him, in the same collection almost equally delicate and beautiful in its marquetry decorations. The diaper patterns so characteristic of this period are most beautifully executed, but are not very interesting, and the mountings take the interest rather from the marquetry, becoming more and more delicately designed and elaborately worked. The principal woods used by Riesener were tulip and rose wood, holly, maple, laburnum, purple wood, and sometimes snake wood. His contemporary, David Roentgen, used principally pear, lime, and light-coloured woods, burnt for the shades.

Plate 49.—*Panel from back of Riesener's bureau, made for Stanislas Leczinski, with figure of Secrecy.*

Plate 50.—*Roundel from bureau, made for Stanislas Leczinski, King of Poland, now in the Wallace Collection.*

Paris has endured a regular invasion of German craftsmen from the middle of the eighteenth century, and the Faubourg S. Antoine still has a number of German-born joiners among its workmen. Among the most celebrated of them was David Roentgen, born either at Neuwied or Herrenhagen in 1743. In 1772 he succeeded his father, Abraham Roentgen, in his business at Neuwied am Rhein, which he had founded in 1753, and from which he retired into the house of the Moravian brethren, where he lived for twenty years longer. The engraver Wille relates that he came to his house in Paris in 1774 with letters of recommendation, and that he put him in touch with designers and sculptors. When Marie Antoinette became Queen he was appointed "Ébéniste méchanicien" to the Queen. He was in such good odour with her as to be charged on several occasions to carry presents to her mother and sisters. Her favour excited the jealousy of the other joiners, and they contested his right to sell foreign-made furniture. He got out of this difficulty by being admitted a member of their corporation on May 24th, 1780. He was so entirely master of his craft, and increased its resources so much by using exotic woods, that contemporary opinion thought it difficult to imagine greater success in the particular direction in which he worked. In 1779 he showed a table of marquetry, made in a new fashion, which he described as a mosaic, "in which the shades are neither burnt, nor engraved, nor darkened with smoke, as one has been obliged to express them until now," a return in fact to the earlier Italian method. His designs were many of them made by Johann Zick of Coblenz, others by Jean Baptiste Le Prince, chinoiseries, and shepherd games. Under him the later German marqueterie reached its highest point. His works went all over Europe, from St. Petersburg to Paris, and replicas were ordered by those who were obliged to forego the originals. He sold to Catherine of Russia a series of articles of furniture for 20,000 roubles, and the Empress added a present of 5000 roubles and a gold snuff-box. The King of Prussia was his constant protector, and in February, 1792, gave him the title of Secret Councillor, and in November of the same year named him Royal Agent on the Lower Rhine. The Revolution ruined him, and he was obliged in 1796 to close his factory. He abandoned France at this period, and the Government, considering him as an "Emigré," seized all his effects in 1793, including the furniture made at Neuwied, then in his stores. He died at Wiesbaden in 1807. With him these incomplete historical notes may terminate. Many of the names mentioned are but names, while in many cases names and works cannot be connected, for the carver and intarsiatori were often, like other craftsmen, content to do the work without caring about the reputation of doing it; but the cases in which facts of the lives or work of these men have been preserved are so much the more interesting from their rarity, and certainly do not show them to any disadvantage compared with other artists, or those among whom their lives were passed.

THE PROCESS OF MANUFACTURE

The early mode of working intarsia in Italy, where it is more than 100 years more ancient than in any other country, was by sinking forms in the wood, according to a prearranged design, and then filling the hollows with pieces of different coloured woods. At first the number of colours used was very small—indeed, Vasari says that the only tints employed were black and white, but this must be interpreted freely, since the colour of wood is not generally uniform, and there would consequently often be a difference in tint in portions cut from different parts of the same plank. A cypress chest of 1350, now in the Victoria and Albert Museum, shows another mode of decoration standing between tarsia proper and the mediæval German and French fashion of sinking the ground round the ornament and colouring it. In this example the design is incised, the ground cleared out to a slight depth, and the internal lines of the drawing and the background spaces filled in with a black mastic, the result much resembling niello. If dark wood be substituted for the mastic background we have almost the effect of the stalls of the chapel of the Palazzo Pubblico at Siena, which, though an early work of Domenico di Nicolò, are well considered in design, well executed, and quite satisfactory in point of harmony between material and design.

Plate 51.—*Antonio Barili at work, by himself.*

At the commencement of the Renaissance the fancy of the intarsiatori overflowed in the most graceful arabesques, which are perfectly suited to the material and are often executed with absolute perfection, and these may perhaps be held to be the most entirely satisfactory of their works, though not the most marvellous. The ambition of the craftsman led him to emulate the achievements of the painter, and we find, after the invention of perspective drawing, views of streets and other architectural subjects, which are not always very successful, and the representation of cupboards, the doors of which are partly open, showing objects of different kinds on the shelves, which are often rendered with the most extraordinary realism, when the means adopted are considered.[3] This realism was much assisted by Fra Giovanni da Verona's discovery of acid solutions and stains for treating the wood, so as to get more variety of colour, and by the practice of scorching portions of the pieces of which the subject was composed, thus suggesting roundness by means of shading. It was a common practice to increase the decorative effect by means of gilding and paint, thus obtaining a brilliancy of colour at the expense of unity of effect sometimes, one may think, if one may judge from the panels in the stalls at the Certosa of Pavia—though perhaps it is scarcely fair to take them as examples of the effect of the older work since they have been restored in modern times. At the best period it was used almost entirely for church furniture and the furnishings of public edifices, in Italy at least, and many of the ranges of stalls still occupy their original positions.

Plate 52.—*Panel from the Victoria and Albert Museum.*

The principal woods used in the work of the best period were pear, walnut, and maple, though pine and cypress also appear. Ebony was imitated with a tincture of gall apples, green was obtained with verdigris, and red with cochineal. Sublimate of mercury, arsenical acid, and sulphuric acid were also used to affect the colour of the wood. This treatment lessened its lasting power, and often caused its decay through the attacks of worms. The scorching was done with molten lead, or in very dark places with a soldering-iron. It is now done with hot sand. The following technical description is taken from a German book of 1669—"Wood-workers paint with quite thin little bits of wood, which are coloured in different ways, and the same are put together after the form of the design in hollowed-out panels, fastened with glue and polished with an iron on the surface so that they may become quite smooth. They paint at the present time in this manner tables and jewel chests or trays, and all in the highest artistic manner. Also separate pictures are put together, which copy the works of the most celebrated masters. First, they take small, very thin pieces of pear or lime dyed through with different colour-stuffs, which are prepared by certain processes, so that the wood is the same colour within and without. Then they give them their several shapes as the kind of picture requires, cutting them according to the size and shape, and stick them with glue on the board. In the place of wood they sometimes use bone, horn, and tortoiseshell cut into fine strips, also ivory and silver. The whole work is called by the Germans 'Einlegen' or 'Furnieren,' because although each piece is separate from the others no part is taken out from the surface in which such figures are inlaid, but the whole is covered." With the use of the fret-saw for cutting the patterns, and the consequent discovery of the possibility of counterchanging the ground and the design (that which was black becoming white, and *vice versâ*), called male and female forms, the manufacture of tarsia, or marquetry rather, commenced to take a more commercial aspect, the cost being considerably reduced by the making of several copies by one sawing. This is the process used at the present day.

The durability of inlaid work depends upon the tightness and completeness with which the inlaid parts are fitted together or mortised into the main body or bed of the wood, and also on the level grounding out of the matrix. In Spanish and Portuguese work ivory or ebony pins or pegs were used also. Marquetry is a form of veneering, and the operation is thus conducted:—The under surface of the veneer and the upper surface of the bed are both carefully levelled and toothed over so as to get a clean, newly-worked surface; the ground is then well wetted with glue, at a high temperature, and the two surfaces pressed tightly together so as to squeeze as much out as possible. The parts are screwed down on heated metal beds, or between wooden frames, made so as to exactly fit the surfaces in every part, called "cauls," until the glue is hard. In cutting the patterns of Boulle work two or three slices of material, such as brass and tortoiseshell or ebony, are glued together with paper between, so that they may be easily separated when the cutting is done. Another piece of paper is glued outside, upon which the pattern is indicated. A fine watch spring saw is then introduced through a hole in an unimportant part of the design, and the patterns sawn out as in ordinary fretwork. The slices are then separated, and that cut out of one slice is fitted into the others so that one cutting produces several repetitions of the design with variations in ground and pattern. When there are only two slices of material the technical term for them is Boulle and Counter. When the various parts have been arranged in their places, face downwards, paper is glued over them to keep the whole in place, and filings of the material rubbed in to fill up any interstices. The whole is then toothed over and laid down in the same manner as ordinary veneer, the ground being first rubbed over with garlic, or some acid, to remove any traces of grease. Marquetry of wood is made in the same way, but more thicknesses of wood are put together to be sawn through, as many as four not being an unusual number, while for common work even eight may be sawn at one time, and the various sheets are pinned together only with a stiff backing of common veneer of good thickness to steady the work. Dye woods are used as far as possible, and holly stained to the required colour serves for greens and blues and a few other tints. Pearl is always cut in one thickness, and is glued down on a backing of wood at least ⅛inch thick.

Another mode of cutting the design approximates more nearly to the ancient practice. The whole design is drawn on paper attached to the ground, or counter, and cut out entirely. The various portions of inlay are then cut from different veneers of the desired colour and fitted into their places. Another method is to paste the paper with the whole design on the ground, and on it to paste the various ornaments cut from suitable veneers, then to cut through the ground, the saw grazing the edges of the ornamental forms. The parts so cut out are then pushed through the ornaments, separated from the paper, and laid down in the vacant places. A variation on this method is to cut out the forms to be inlaid in different veneers, and glue them in their proper positions on a sheet of paper. A sheet of white paper is pasted on the veneer, which is to serve as the ground. A sheet of blackened paper is laid over it, and over this the sheet with the forms to be inlaid, which are then struck with a light mallet, so as to print an impression of their edges upon the paper. The printed shapes are then cut out one at a time, care being taken to make the saw exactly follow the outline. The object of all these processes is, of course, to ensure the ground and the inlaid forms exactly fitting. After cleaning the surface from paper and glue it is smoothed with plane and scraper, and the markings on leaves or other figures made by a graver, if not already made by saw cuts, and they and the lines between the male and female forms are filled with shellac or wood-dust and glue.

In Germany the veneers used are one to two millimetres thick, *i.e.*, one-twenty-fifth or two-twenty-fifths of an inch. The principal woods used are walnut, pear, ash, bird maple, holly, olive, amboyna, rose wood, violet wood, thuya, and palisander, which name is also used on the Continent for rose wood and violet, though it is really a sort of cedar. Tortoiseshell, ivory, and metal plates are also used, principally of pewter, brass, and zinc. Seeman's Kunstgewerbliche Handbücher advise thus:—"When ivory or hard precious metals are used it is better to divide the design into smaller parts. To avoid damage to the effect by time and change of colour in the woods such combinations as the following are to be preferred:—Mahogany and black walnut, pear and black walnut, Hungarian ash and black thuya, pear and palisander, brass and black, etc. For fine, small ornament smooth, even-textured woods should be used such as pear, mahogany, maple, or holly; for broad patches and backgrounds, which are not required to be dark, you should use patterned or streaked woods, like bird maple, amboyna, thuya, or olive. Ivory, mother-of-pearl, and metals in large pieces look hard and loud, so it is better to use them in quite small pieces. If engraved, larger pieces may be employed and used for inscription tablets, coats of arms, and cartouches, or for bits of figures, birds, and butterflies. Shading may be done in various ways. Lines may be engraved and filled up with a glue cement, or hatchings may be drawn with a scorching solution, or the wood may be burnt with hot sand. The sand is made hot in an iron pot, and the piece to be darkened inserted. Or it may be scorched with a hot iron or spirit or gas flame. The simplest way is with the poker used in poker work." In England the sand is heaped upon a metal plate which is heated underneath. The veneer is held with tweezers and pushed into the sand, the gradation of heat giving gradation of tone. The hot sand shrinks the wood, and allowance must be made for this.

Veneers are both saw and knife cut; the saw wastes about as much as the thickness cut in sawdust. They range from 8 to 15 to the inch. The French saw-cut their veneers thinner than the English do.

The woods in every-day use at the present day are white holly, box, pear (in various shades), and holly (dyed all colours); while the veneer merchants sometimes supply also planetree, sycamore, chestnut, Brazilwood, yellow fustic, barwood, tulipwood, kingwood, East and West India satinwood, rosewood, ebony, ash, harewood, Indian purplewood, hornbeam, and snakewood. Bird's-eye maple and partridgewood may also be bought.

Dye woods used for marquetry—Braziletto, cam wood, logwood, Nicaragua, red sanders, sapan, ebony, fustic (a species of mulberry), Zante (a species of sumach). "Ebony is the black pear tree of Madagascar, at least they make cider of its fruit." So says M. Luchet in an interesting excursus on furniture manufacture in his book on the Paris Exhibition of 1867, in which he gives further details of ancient manufacture and its modern imitation. "I know a factory," he says, "where the tortoiseshell is false, the mother-of-pearl false, the ivory holly wood; the brass is the only real thing, because science applied to industry has not yet found out how to imitate it. When Boulle employed wood in his work it was ebony—they have abandoned that for blackened pear wood, under the pretext that ebony is a hard, close wood which twists, splits, and cracks, takes glue badly, and refuses varnish. So that they call a man who never uses ebony 'ébéniste.' They did not trouble about these things in the time of Louis XIV. They never varnished their furniture, so it did not matter that ebony would not take varnish.... There are two sorts of tortoiseshell, that of the Antilles, often bad and scaly, but good enough for common work, because it is thin and equal in thickness, and a little carmine vermilion gives it a not unpleasant red tint. The Indian tortoiseshell is thick and opaque and unequal, demanding preparation and welding. It can only be used for expensive work, and takes easily a black preparation which makes it magnificently austere." One ought to mention here that good shell was often treated with carmine vermilion or with gold, and that without a colour background it loses half its beauty and value.

"In modern times six or eight couples of shell and metal are sawn together, whereas two was the number in the fine period. This saves money. A new Boulle bed, secretary, or chest of drawers should cost 15 to 20,000 francs. You may easily get one for 2000 made of rubbish. An honest chest of drawers with tolerable mountings is worth 1500 francs. In gelatine tortoiseshell and brass or zinc of the future 100 is the price.... The mode still practised in Paris of making a good 'placage' in preparation for marquetry or Boulle work is as follows:—A thicker or thinner sheet of Italian poplar is placed between two sheets of oak with the grain the other way, then on the external sheet of oak is placed the wood intended to be seen, also with the grain the other way, the whole of convenient thickness, and glued with the best glue. Good glue is the nurse of the wood, say the masters. These four or five thicknesses of wood pulling against each other neutralise all bad effects, and the result is very good. The external covering is usually either mahogany, American walnut, or violet wood (a sort of cedar). Sometimes it is ebony, or perhaps a collection of small pieces of wood, such as acacia, which are called by all sorts of pretty names. It is of this fine and good 'plaqué' that they still make cupboards at 1000 francs, beds at 600 francs, and bureaus at 800 francs, which are the success and the pride of Parisian joinery." The marqueteurs of Nice made use of olive for veined grey backgrounds, orange and lemon for pale yellow, carob for dark red, jujube tree for rose colour, holly for white, and charred fig for black; arbutus served for dark flesh, and sumach for light.

It is advisable after the marquetry has been put together to reduce the surface to a level and do something in the way of polishing, though it is not necessary to carry the process as far as is often done by the cheap furniture manufacturers. If nothing but wood has been used, the surface should be reduced to a level with a toothing plane and scraped with a joiner's scraper, taking care to apply it obliquely to the joints as far as possible, so as to avoid digging down and so failing in the object aimed at. If done very well and carefully it sometimes only requires to be rubbed down with its own shavings, but it is more usually necessary to follow with a worn piece of glass-paper on a flat piece of cork, but the dust must not be allowed to collect into hard lumps upon it, as these lumps would scratch the surface.

Holtzapffel says that when metal, ivory, pearl, shell, or tortoiseshell are mixed with the wood the surface must be carefully levelled with flat files, ending with a very smooth one, after which the scraper should be used if possible and followed by glass or emery paper very sparingly. When metal preponderates emery paper is best, and really good *sand* paper may also be used, but all paper should have very little "cut," should be applied dry, and allowed to become clogged, so as to act principally as a hard dry rubber or burnisher. If the polishing is at all in excess the wood will get rubbed or worn down below the metal. The fine finish required when tortoiseshell and metal are used is got by rubbing with blocks of charcoal used endways with oil and the finest rotten-stone powder, much like polishing marble, using oil instead of water. Wet polishing should not be used for inlaid works; the water may soften the glue. A superficial wetting is likely to warp the woods and make them curl up at the edges, and the grain of the wood is almost certain to rise. Oil is better than water, but light woods are almost certain to become stained by polishing powders and fluid. To avoid this modern marquetry is often covered with varnish applied with friction like French polish, or laid on in several coats with a brush and polished off with pumice and rotten stone, like the Vernis Martin, being first levelled with a file or scraper and smoothed with glass-paper.

THE LIMITATIONS AND CAPABILITIES OF THE ART

The process described, by which the early works in intarsia were produced, was slow and tedious; and, as may be supposed, though fame might be won by its exercise, the winning of fortune was a very different thing. Domenico di Nicolò, who made the stalls in the chapel of the Palazzo Pubblico, Siena, and was thence called "del Coro," or "dei Cori," a name which descended to his children in place of their proper name of Spinelli, is an example in point. The petitions to the priors already referred to, printed in Milanesi's Documenti per la Storia dell' Arte Senese, show how little a man of talent, who was constantly employed for many years and gained great reputation in his art, could do to provide for his old age; and many returns of both painters, sculptors, and woodworkers, made for the purposes of taxation and printed in the same book, show that even in a great and flourishing town like Siena, which prided itself on its artistic reputation, it was often most difficult for the craftsmen, on whose work that reputation was based, to make a living.[4] It is true that there were thirty-four workshops for wood carving and intarsia in Florence at one time (1478, as Fabroni says in his life of Lorenzo the Magnificent), from which one may conclude that work of a certain sort was plentiful and lucrative, and panels of intarsia were certainly sometimes exported, but it may be observed that all the most celebrated intarsiatori practised some other form of art also, and generally abandoned intarsia sooner or later;

the exceptions being those who belonged to the Olivetan and Dominican orders, and therefore had no anxiety about their living. Of these craftsmen the most celebrated were Fra Giovanni da Verona and Fra Damiano of Bergamo, whose works were so elaborate and so finely executed as to excite the suspicion that they were painted with the brush, though supposed to be executed with wood and the chisel. The anecdote of the Emperor Charles V.'s trial of Fra Damiano's tarsia panel in S. Domenico, Bologna, attests the wonderful quality of the work, and its success in attaining a doubtful aim, and Barili's inscription in the panel showing himself at work shows that it was not uncommon for such panels to be supposed to be the work of the brush. The designs from which the intarsia was executed were often furnished by painters of repute, and pictures or portions of pictures were copied, a proceeding which Fra Giovanni's discovery of stains and washes of different kinds made easier, until the proper limits of the art were far overpassed, and its decorative quality quite lost sight of in the attempt to rival a form of art the requirements of which were quite different. The beautiful arabesques, which the designers of the early Renaissance poured forth with exhaustless fertility, show the capabilities of the process for decorating flat surfaces, and the perspectives of cupboards and buildings were often most successful without passing the limits imposed by the material.

The question of the limits within which the craftsman's effort should be confined in any form of art craftsmanship is a thorny one, for the attempt to overstep those limits has always had attractions for the craftsman who is master of his craft, and who sighs for fresh fields to conquer, knowing better than the outsider what are the difficulties which he has overcome successfully in any piece of work from the side of craftsmanship, though often with disastrous results when the matter is regarded from the point of view of excellence in design and purity of taste. It has been maintained by purists in modern times that all engraving or shading of the pieces of wood used in forming the design is illegitimate; and if this be so, it is equally illegitimate to stain any of them; but it is undeniable that a great addition to the resources of the inlayer was made by the discoveries of Fra Giovanni, and it seems unreasonable to refuse to make any use of them because later intarsiatori abused these means of gaining effect. The earliest work, it is true, depends mainly upon silhouette for its beauty, but does not altogether disdain lines within the main outline, and the abandonment of these inner lines, whether made by graver or saw, so reduces the possibilities of choice of subject as to restrict the designer to a simplicity which is apt to become bald. A great deal may be done by choice of pieces of wood and arrangement of the direction of the lines of the grain; some of Fra Giovanni's perspectives show very suggestive skies made in this manner, and Fra Damiano was very successful in thus suggesting the texture of much veined and coloured marble and of rocks, but directly the human figure enters into the design these expedients are felt to be insufficient and inexpressive, and inner lines have perforce to be introduced. The opposite extreme is such work as the panels by the brothers Caniana in the Colleoni Chapel at Bergamo, in which the composition and drawing of the figures recall the designs of the Caracci, and the technique of the shading reminds one of a copper plate, while the tinting and gradation of the colours take away all impression of a work in wood, substituting that of a coloured engraving. Here it is quite evident that the desire to imitate pictorial qualities has led the craftsman far away from what should have been his aim, viz., to display the qualities of the material which he was using to the best advantage, consistently with the position and purpose of his work in it. Not that perfection of workmanship is to be decried, though it is only occasionally that one is able to make use of, or indeed produce it. But the æsthetic sense demands that consideration for material and purpose in every production which the joy and pride of the craftsman in overcoming difficulties sometimes prevents him from giving. Notwithstanding the beauty of much of the marquetry of the periods of Louis XIV. and Louis XV., one often feels that design has been put to one side in the endeavour to gain a realistic effect, and the same defect may be traced more clearly in the clumsier Dutch and German productions. Even in the Italian work of an earlier date every now and then the same fault peeps out, though the excellent taste of the nation at that period prevented the Italians from falling into such excesses, and one generally feels the wood even in their most elaborate perspectives. It may be asserted in a general way that the more colours are used the less likelihood is there of the effect being quite satisfactory, and that any light and shade introduced should be of the simplest kind. A slight darkening of parts of the wood to gain a certain suggestion of roundness is quite admissible, but the expedient should be used with discretion, lavish employment of it leading to heaviness of effect and a monotony of tone which are most unpleasing. If ivory or metals are introduced the greatest care is necessary to prevent them from giving a spotty and uneven effect to the design, for neither these two materials nor mother-of-pearl marry quite with the tone of the wood; and this inequality is likely to increase with age, as the wood becomes richer and mellower in colour. Such materials should be so used that the points where they occur may form a pattern in themselves independently of the rest of the design, so that the effect may be pleasing at first sight, before the general meaning of the less prominent details is realised. Any other way of using them courts failure, since the effect of the whole design is ruined by the uncalculated prominence and inequality of these materials here and there. The Dutch sometimes made use of mother-of-pearl, in pieces upon which engraving broke up the hard glitter of the material, mingled with brass wire and nails or studs driven into the surface of the wood. The two materials appear to be quite harmonious, and small articles decorated in this manner are effective and satisfactory. The Italian use of ivory for the decoration of musical instruments, chess and backgammon boards, and other small objects is almost always successful, the proportion between wood and ivory being well judged, and the forms of the ornament pleasing.

Plate 53.—*Panel from S. Maria in Organo, Verona.*

The modern French marquetry, though exceedingly clever and beautiful in its use of various woods, errs by want of consideration of the surface to be decorated, the subjects flowing over the surfaces and overflowing the proper boundaries very often; and also sins in using many woods of very slightly different tones and textures, which will almost certainly lose their reciprocal relation in the course of time, and thereby their decorative effect. The ancient intarsias were made of a small number of different woods, and the effect was kept simple; pear, white poplar, oak, walnut, and holly almost exhaust the list; while even Roentgen's work, in which he used a larger number of woods, including some of those foreign trees which Dutch commerce made available for him, has suffered from their changing and fading. I would advise the marqueteur to disregard most of the many foreign woods now in the market, and content himself with simple and well-proved effects for the most part, trusting rather to beauty of design to give distinction to his work than to variety of colour and startling effects of contrast.

Plate 54.—*Panel from S. Maria in Organo, Verona.*

It is the fashion at the present day to exhort the designer to found his design upon the study of nature, which is right enough if accompanied by discretion and a feeling for style. In many mouths, however, the exhortation means that the copying of natural forms is advised, and often, if one may judge from the examples which one sees around one, without selection either of subject or form. Now it is obvious that it is sometimes the beauty of form in natural objects which attracts the eye, and sometimes the beauty or strangeness of colours, either in their combination or from the unusual tint. And while the former quality fits the object for translation into ornament, by means of simplification and repetition, the latter is more likely to be the suggestive starting point for the production of something quite different than a factor in a directly-derived composition. Certain forms of flowers and leaves are also suitable for ornament expressed in a certain way, and when this harmony occurs the representation of nature is satisfactory as ornament; but the reverse is very often shown to be the case in work of a more modern type, in which the design is based on the dictum that the copying of natural forms will produce ornament. It is not the copying of natural forms, but the ordering of the spaces, the arranging and balancing of line and mass, and the adaptation of means to ends which produce satisfactory decoration, and in the best Italian intarsias founded upon freely-growing, natural plants this is well shown. The observation of natural growth shown in illustrations Nos. 53, 54, and 55 is considerable, but the panels are not so beautiful because the bay, the pink, or the lily are so well rendered, but because the pattern of waving lines is so well fitted to the space it has to fill, and the shapes of the silhouettes are so expressive. In the later French marquetry we often find an equal or almost equal dexterity in expressing the natural form, and an almost greater cleverness in adapting the design to the material; but the Italian work has a fineness of style shown in a grace of arrangement and of proportioning the ornament to the space to be filled which is unsurpassable.

Certain remarks made by Mr. Stephen Webb, in a paper read to the Society of Arts on April 28, 1899, as to the qualities which the designer or craftsman must possess for successfully producing intarsia, are worth reproducing here as the sayings of a man who himself has done much beautiful work of the kind. "Tone harmony, and in a limited degree, the sense of values, he must certainly cultivate. He must be able to draw a line or combination of lines which *may* be ingenious if you like, but *must* be delicate and graceful, vigorous withal, and in proper relation to any masses which he may introduce into his design. He must thoroughly understand the value of contrast in line and surface form, but these matters, though a stumbling block to the amateur, are the opportunities of the competent designer and craftsman. The most charming possibilities of broken colour lie ready to his hand, to be merely selected by him and introduced into his design. If the wood be properly selected shading is rarely necessary, and if it is done at all should be done by an artist. In the hands of an artist very beautiful effects may be obtained, the same kind of wood being made to yield quite a number of varying shades of colour of a low but rich tone. Over-staining and the abuse of shading are destructive. Ivory has always been a favourite material with workers in tarsia, and in the hands of an experienced designer very charming things may be done with it. There is, however, no material suitable for tarsia which requires so much care and experience in its use. It is ineffective in light-coloured woods, and in the darker ordinary woods, such as ebony, stained mahogany, or rosewood, under polish, the contrast of colour is so great that the ivory must be used very sparingly. The ivory is sometimes stained in order to bring its colour more into harmony with a dark wood-ground, but it is never quite satisfactory. The use of inlay makes the direction from which the light enters the room a matter of no moment, so long as the light reaches the object decorated."

The effect of intarsia has been sought by various imitative processes, some of which are indistinguishable from it except by close inspection. In one of these wax, either in its natural state or tinted with an addition of powder colour, was used; in another glue mixed with whiting or plaster, also sometimes tinged, or red lead. On April 7, 1902, a paper was read at the Royal Institute of British Architects on wax stoppings of this kind by Mr. Heywood Sumner, in the course of which he said that the process he himself had used was as follows:— "First trace the design on the panel of wood to be incised; cut it, either with a V tool or knife blade fixed in a tool-handle; clear out the larger spaces with a small gouge, leaving tool-mark roughness in the bottoms for key; when cut, stop the suction of the wood by several coats of white, hard polish. For coloured stoppings, resin (as white as can be got), beeswax, and powdered distemper are the three things needful. The melted wax may be run into the incisions by means of a small funnel with handle and gas jet affixed; it is attachable to the nearest gas burner by india-rubber tubing, so that a regulated heat can be applied to the funnel. When thus attached and heated, pieces of wax of the required inlay colour are dropped into the funnel, and soon there will be a run of melted wax dropping from the end of the funnel-spout, which is easily guided by means of the wooden handle, and thus the entire panel may be inlaid with the melted wax. Superfluous surface wax is cleared off with a broad chisel, so as to make the whole surface flush. The suction of the wood is stopped by means of white, hard polish, otherwise the hot wax will enter the grain of the wood and stain it. Incised panels may be filled successfully with japanner's gold size and powdered distemper colour, using a palette knife to distribute the slab mixture. A close grain is the one thing needful in the wood. As to design, that which is best suited may be compared to a broad sort of engraving." Red lead was also used sometimes, and in the furniture room at South Kensington there are several chests and other pieces of furniture which have the incised design filled in with a mixture of whiting, glue, and linseed oil.

Plate 55.—*Panel from S. Pietro in Casinense, Perugia.*

At Hardwick some of the door panels are painted with arabesques in Indian ink, and varnished (a process also employed on several pieces of furniture in the South Kensington collection), and even in certain cases, no doubt under the direction of Bess of Hardwick, engravings have been stuck on the panels, tinted, surrounded with similar painting, and then similarly varnished over. The sacristy cupboards at S. Maria delle

Grazie, Milan, called "Lo Scaffale," show paintings of no less an artist than Luini, the ornamental part of which is intended to simulate tarsia.

For small objects, such as trinket boxes, a marquetry of straw tinted to different colours was sometimes employed, which, though not very lasting, in the hands of a worker who possessed taste in colour sometimes produced pleasing results, a form of work practised both in Holland and England, and lasting well into the 19th century. The writer possesses one or two objects decorated by this process which were bought from the French prisoners taken in the Peninsular War, who provided themselves with little luxuries by making and selling them. In all these imitative processes the question of design becomes of the very highest importance, since the material has neither beauty nor intrinsic value in itself; and here, even more than in many other forms of manufacture, the presence and influence of the intelligent designer is most desirable, and should be paramount.

WORKSHOP RECEIPTS

The use of stains and chemical baths for changing the colour of the wood employed by the intarsiatori was common from the time of Fra Giovanni da Verona, to whom Vasari ascribes the invention, but is most distinctive of the work of the later Dutch and French marqueteurs. Receipts for the purpose were handed down from master to pupil, and while sometimes held as traditional secrets to be jealously guarded, were sometimes committed to writing; and several of these manuscripts have come down to us. The following have been collected from French, German, and Italian sources, and though not all of equal value, show the way in which the ancient workers produced the effects, most of which we admire in the present day:—

To stain wood yellow (No. 1).—Put saffron in water, and when it is well steeped place the jar over hot coals. Then spread the stuff over boxwood with a brush. To make it brilliant let it dry, and put it with oil on the wood to be coloured. (No. 2.)—Take the plant turmeric (curcuma longa), grind it to powder; put an ounce into a pint of spirit (12 oz.), and leave it for a day. If the tone is required reddish, add some dragon's blood. (No. 3.)—A cheaper but duller colour is to be obtained from steeped French berries, then dried, with weak alum water brushed over it. Thin pieces are dipped in it. The solution of French berries may be made thus—Take 1 lb. of French berries, and a gallon of water with ½ oz. of alum; boil for an hour in a pewter vessel, and filter through paper. Evaporate till the colour appears strong enough. Another receipt says 4 oz. of French berries put to steep in a pint of water is to have added to it 1 oz. of hazel nuts and as much alum. Wood may also be stained yellow with *aqua fortis*, used warm, and then immediately placed near the fire. The *aqua fortis* must not be too strong, or the wood will go brown or black. This is apparently the same thing as Vasari calls "oil of sulphur," used in his time for colouring wood. A Nuremberg receipt book says that the plant Tournesol (croton tinctorium) may be steeped in water, and this solution mixed with yellow colour and glue may be spread over the wood warm, and finally polished with a burnisher. Holtzapffel gives the following:—A bright yellow stain may be obtained from 2 oz. of turmeric allowed to simmer for some hours in 1 quart of water in an earthen vessel, water being added from time to time to replace evaporation. Sparingly applied cold, it stains white woods the colour of satin wood. A canary yellow results from immersing the wood in the liquid, which can be rendered permanent without polishing by a strong solution of common salt. Washing the stained surface with nitro-muriate of tin for about a minute changes the colour to orange. The work should then be well rinsed in plain water to check the further action of the acid. Treating the canary yellow with 2 oz. of sulphate of iron dissolved in 3 quarts of water, after it has been allowed to dry, dyes a delicate olive brown. A tincture of ¼ oz. of turmeric to 3 oz. of spirits of wine, allowed to stand for some days and well shaken daily, gives a rather higher colour.

Red may be produced by (No. 1) taking a pound of Brazil wood, with some rain water, a handful of unslaked lime, and two handsful of ashes; soak all for half an hour in water, "cook" it, and pour it out into another pot, in which is a measure of gum arabic. The wood to be coloured must be cooked in alum water, and then brushed over with the warm colour; the result is a splendid scarlet red. If the wood was first grounded with saffron water and then had the Brazil decoction applied, the result was orange; a spoonful of lye made a browner colour, with a little alum. If whiter wood was taken the colour was correspondingly brighter. (No. 2.)—Orcanda or Akanna root powdered, with nut oil, gives a fine red. (No. 3.)—Put lime in rain water, strain it, scrape Brazil twigs in it, then proceed as in No. 1. You can also soak the Brazil in tartar. The same colour with Tournesol steeped in water gives a fine purple when spread on the wood. Lebrun gives the same receipt, adding that the beauty of the colour is increased by rubbing with oil, and that pear wood is the best to use. Another receipt says:—Make a strong infusion of Brazil wood in stale urine or water impregnated with pearl ash, 1 oz. to a gallon; to a gallon of either of which put 1 lb. of Brazil wood. Let it stand for two or three days, often stirring it. Strain the infusion, and brush over the wood boiling hot; then, while still wet, brush over with alum water, 2 oz. to a quart of water. A less bright red may be made with 1 oz. of dragon's blood in a pint of spirits of wine, brushed over the wood.

Holtzapffel gives for red stains the following:—Dragon's blood, an East Indian resin, gives a crimson with a purple tinge. Put a small quantity in an open vessel, and add sufficient linseed oil to rather more than cover it; it will be fit for use in a few days, when the oil may be poured off and more added. This dissolves more readily in oil than spirit. The colouring matter of Alkanet root, from which another red may be obtained, is contained in the rind, so that small pieces are the most useful. A deep red of a crimson character may be made with ½ oz. of raspings of Brazil wood macerated in 3 oz. of alcohol. A wash of logwood (see below) given with the brush, and when dry followed with a wash of Brazil, produces a deep, full colour, and when the two are applied in the reverse order a more brilliant colour of the same kind. A decoction of Brazil (4 oz.) allowed to simmer for some hours in 1 quart of water yields a rather brown-red stain. Treating light woods so stained with nitro-muriate of tin gives a brilliant crimson of a purple tinge.

A brown red is made from a decoction of 2 oz. of logwood dust in 1 quart of water, or ½ oz. of logwood in 3 oz. of alcohol. Nitro-muriate of tin used on it gives a deep, dusky crimson purple. The same treated with alum solution yields a medium purple, darker and bluer than that from Brazil.

White wood stained with Brazil and then treated with alum (4 oz. dissolved in a quart of water) acquires a light pink tinge. Another receipt for pink or rose red says:—1 gallon of infusion of Brazil wood, with 2 oz. additional of pearl ash; but it is necessary to brush the wood often with alum water. By increasing the proportion of pearl ash the red may be made still paler, in which case make the alum water stronger.

For purple one brushes the wood over several times with a strong decoction of logwood and Brazil, 1 lb. of logwood and ¼ lb. of Brazil to a gallon of water boiled for an hour or more. When the wood is dark enough let it dry, and then lightly pass over with a solution of 1 drachm of pearl ash to a quart of water. Use this carefully, as the colour changes quickly from brown red to dark purple.

Jet black may be made by using the logwood stain, followed by a solution of iron, 1 oz. sulphate of iron to 1 quart of water, and a less intense black by the same mixture about three times diluted. The Italian receipt books are well provided with receipts for producing black, which suggests that most of the ebony used in inlay was factitious. A 15th century MS. says:—"Take boxwood, and lay in oil with sulphur for a night, then let it stew for an hour, and it will become as black as coal." Evidently this means what Vasari calls oil of sulphur, *aqua fortis*. Others are founded upon the application of a solution of logwood, followed by one of iron. "Stew logwood till the liquid is reduced to one-third of its bulk, mix with stone alum, and leave for three days. Mix iron filings with very strong wine, and let it stand for twenty-four hours. On the quantity of iron filings the depth of the tone depends. Lastly, ox-gall is dissolved in this mixture, and the whole is three times worked over." An English receipt says:—"Brush the wood over several times with a hot decoction of logwood; take ¼ lb. of powdered galls, and set in the sun or other gentle heat in 2 quarts of water for three or four days; brush the wood over with it three or four times, and, while wet, with a solution of green vitriol in water, 2 oz. to a quart; or use a solution of copper in *aqua fortis*, then the solution of logwood, and repeat until black enough." A German receipt says:—"Take half a measure of iron filings and a pennyweight of sal ammoniac, and put into a pot of vinegar; let it stand for twelve days at least. In another pot put blue Brazil and 3 measures of bruised gall apples in strong lime lye, and let it stand for the same time. The wood must be first washed over with lye, and then with hot vinegar, and finally polished with wax." "Pear wood may be grounded with Brazil steeped in alum water, then coloured with the black which the leather-stainers use, twenty times." Another says:—"Take a pennyweight of fine silver, with a pound of *aqua fortis*; add a measure of water, and soak the wood with it." The best wood for imitating ebony is holly; also, box cooked in olive oil is good for it, or well-planed pear soaked with *aqua fortis*, and then coloured with ink several times; or stew the wood in lamp-black, and soak with oil.

Blue may be obtained by the use of a solution of copper brushed hot over the wood several times; then brush hot a solution of pearl ash, 2 oz. to a pint of water, until the wood becomes perfectly blue. The copper solution is prepared in this way:—"Take of the refiner's solution of copper made in the precipitation of silver from the spirit of nitre; or dissolve copper in spirit of nitre, or *aqua fortis*, by throwing in filings or putting in strips of copper gradually till all effervescence ceases. Add to it starch finely powdered, one-fifth or one-sixth of the weight of copper dissolved. Make a solution of pearl ash and filter it; put gradually to the solution of copper as much as will precipitate the whole of the copper. The fluid becomes colourless. Wash the powder, and when so well drained of water by means of a filter as to be of the proper consistence, grind well together, and lay out to dry. This makes dark verditer." Indigo may also be used, prepared with soap lees as when used by dyers; brush it over the wood boiling hot. With a solution of cream of tartar, 3 oz. to a quart of water, and boiled, brush over the wood copiously before the moisture is quite dried out. A German receipt says:—Put 4 oz. of Tournesol in three parts of lime water to cook for an hour and spread it on the wood. "Wood coloured green with verdigris can be made blue by using pearl ash." This is the process described first.

For green verdigris dissolved in vinegar may be used; or crystals of verdigris in water, brushed hot over the wood. A 15th century MS. gives a traditional mode thus:—"Wood, bone, small leaves, and knife handles can be made green by strong, red vinegar and brass filings mixed together with a little Roman vitriol and stone alum in a glass vessel. When it has stood for a day the object is dipped in it, and steeps itself in the liquid. The colour will be very permanent." A German receipt says:—"Take walnut shells from the green fruit, and put in very strong lye with some copper vitriol and alum to stew for two or three hours. The wood must be put in strong wine vinegar for several days, then it is put in the above-mentioned mixture, to which ground verdigris mixed with vinegar is added. Or you can mix this ground verdigris with vinegar with some winestone, let it clarify, and spread the wood with the filtered stuff. The addition of saffron makes a grass green."

A silver grey may be given to white wood by immersion in a decoction of 4 oz. of sumach in 1 quart of water, and afterwards in a very dilute solution of sulphate of iron. A dilute solution of bichromate of potash is frequently employed to darken oak, mahogany, and coloured woods. This should be used carefully, since its effects are not altogether stopped by thoroughly washing the wood with water when dark enough. To bleach woods, immerse them in a strong, hot solution of oxalic acid.

Since ivory is often used in inlaying and is sometimes stained, a few receipts for its staining will not be out of place. These come from Holtzapffel's book:— A pale yellow will be given by immersing the ivory for one minute in the tepid stain given by 60 grains of saffron boiled for some hours in half-a-pint of water. Immersion for from five to fifteen minutes produces a canary yellow brighter or deeper according to the time given, but all somewhat fugitive. A stain from 4 oz. of fustic dust and chips boiled in 1 quart of water produces similar but somewhat darker and more permanent results. Ivory subjected to either of these stains for fifteen minutes, and then placed for one to three minutes in Brazil water stain acquires an orange colour. If then treated with nitro-muriate of tin, an orange of a brighter, redder tone is produced; transfer to a clean water bath directly the required colour appears, as the nitro-muriate of tin acts very rapidly upon the ivory.

Fine scarlet cloth is used for dyeing various tones of red. A piece about a foot square may be cut into shreds and boiled, with the addition of 10 grains of pearl ash, in half-a-pint of water from 5 to 6 hours. Immersion in the liquid for from three to ten minutes gives tones of pink; for one hour and subsequently for half-an-hour in an alum mordant gives a pink of a bright crimson character. When the ivory is from two to three hours in the tepid stain a crimson red results, and the addition of 1 part of sulphuric acid to 60 of stain gives billiard ball colour. Pinks of a different and duller full tone may be obtained by immersion for three minutes in Brazil water stain, followed by treatment with nitro-muriate of tin; when the Brazil is used for six minutes a deeper colour results. Fifteen minutes in Brazil, then treatment with nitro-muriate of tin and immediate washing gives a duller and deeper red than the first red-cloth stain. The depth of colour may be increased by longer immersion *or* a higher temperature. A dull scarlet or brick red is made by the Brazil bath, followed by thirty to sixty minutes in an alum mordant.

The cloth stain for one hour, followed by pearl ash for half-an-hour, gives a bright purple; if iron is used instead of pearl ash a sombre purple results; if you add alkalies to the stain instead of sulphuric acid you obtain purple reds. Fifteen minutes in Brazil, and then three or four in pearl ash gives full red purples deepening to maroon. Five minutes in logwood water stain gives a good warm brown; half-an-hour, a chocolate brown. Ten minutes in logwood stain, washing, and one or two seconds in pearl ash, and instantly washing again gives a deep red brown, and if one minute in alum instead of pearl ash a deep purple brown.

Blue stains may be made from sulphate of indigo, ½ drachm to 1 pint of previously boiled water, with 10 grains of carbonate of potash added. One to two minutes' immersion and immediate washing yields a delicate turquoise, five minutes a bright full blue; and ten to fifteen a considerable depth of colour. Blues are rather fugitive. Staining with saffron or fustic for five minutes, and then with indigo for the same time, produces a clear pea green; with indigo for ten minutes, a deep grass green. The greens from fustic are more permanent and yellower. The sequence of the stains also affects the green, the last used having most effect. Blue stain first for fifteen minutes, followed by fustic for thirty, stains ivory the green used for table knife handles—a colour which may also be obtained by immersion for some weeks in a clear solution of verdigris in dilute vinegar and water.

Before applying these stains the ivory must be prepared by first polishing with whiting and water and washing quite clean. Next immerse it for three to five minutes in acid cold water (1 part muriatic acid to 40 or 50 of water, or the same proportion of nitric). This extracts the gelatine from the surface of the ivory. Extreme cleanliness and absence of grease or soiling is most important; the ivory is not to be touched by the fingers, but removed from one vessel to another by wooden tongs, one pair to each colour. After treating with the acid, place the ivory in clean, cold, boiled water for some minutes. Water stains are used, but strained or filtered and warm or only tepid, for fear of injuring the surface of the ivory. Increasing the temperature also sometimes deepens or changes the colour. The best temperature is 100 deg. Fahr. When sufficiently stained the ivory is well rinsed in water, and if there are two colours on top of each other always well rinsed before going into the second bath. After thoroughly drying, repolish by friction, first with a few drops of oil on a soft clean rag; continue with a dry clean rag till the oil disappears.

An old Italian receipt for polishing wood blackened to imitate ebony runs thus:—"Is the wood to be polished with burnt pumice stone? Rub the work carefully with canvas and this powder, then wash the piece with Dutch lime water so that it may be more beautifully polished. Then it is to be cleaned with another cloth. Then the rind of a pomegranate must be steeped, and the wood smeared over with it and set to dry, but in the shade."

FOOTNOTES:

[1] Pliny, Book 16, Chap. 83—"Glue, too, plays one of the principal parts in all veneering and works of marquetry. For this purpose the workmen usually employ wood with a threaded vein, to which they give the name of 'ferulea,' from its resemblance to the grain of the giant fennel, this part of the wood being preferred from its being dotted and wavy." Chap. 84—"The wood, too, of the beech is easily worked, although it is brittle and soft. Cut into thin layers of veneer it is very flexible, but is only used for the construction of boxes and desks. The wood, too, of the holm oak is cut into veneers of remarkable thinness, the colour of which is far from unsightly; but it is more particularly where it is exposed to friction that this wood is valued, as being one to be depended upon; in the axle trees of wheels, for instance, for which the ash is also employed, on account of its pliancy, the holm oak for its hardness, and the elm for the union in it of both these qualities.... The best woods for cutting into layers and employing as a veneer for covering others are the citrus, the terebinth, the different varieties of the maple, the box, the palm, the holly, the holm oak, the root of the elder, and the poplar. The alder furnishes, also, a kind of tuberosity, which is cut into layers like those of the citrus and the maple. In all the other trees, the tuberosities are of no value whatever. It is the central part of trees that is most variegated, and the nearer we approach to the root the smaller are the spots and the more wavy. It was in this appearance that originated that requirement of luxury

which displays itself in covering one tree with another, and bestowing upon the more common woods a bark of higher price. In order to make a single tree sell many times over laminæ of veneer have been devised; but that was not thought sufficient—the horns of animals must next be stained of different colours, and their teeth cut into sections, in order to decorate wood with ivory, and, at a later period, to veneer it all over. Then, after all this, man must go and seek his materials in the sea as well! For this purpose he has learned to cut tortoise shell into sections; and of late, in the reign of Nero, there was a monstrous invention devised of destroying its natural appearance by paint, and making it sell at a still higher price by a successful imitation of wood.

"It is in this way that the value of our couches is so greatly enhanced; it is in this way, too, that they bid the rich lustre of the terebinth to be outdone, a mock citrus to be made that shall be more valuable than the real one, and the grain of the maple to be feigned. At one time luxury was not content with wood; at the present day it sets us on buying tortoise shells in the guise of wood."—Pliny's Natural History, Bohn's Translation.

[2] There were nineteen subjects, divided by channelled pilasters with a carved frieze, above a bench which ran round the circular wall from one doorpost to the other, the whole work crowned with a cornice also carved with foliated ornament. The first subject on the right was an open cupboard with architects' and joiners' tools. The second was the portrait described above. The

third showed a cupboard half open, worked with a grille of pierced almond shapes and divided. "In the upper part is a naked boy, standing with a ball in his left hand, below is a large circle with a bridge within and without in the form of a diamond. Within the closed part of the grille one sees a ewer above and a basin below. The fourth is a figure of S. Ansano, half-length, below whom is the head of a man who receives baptism with joined hands, and the saint with a vase in his hand pours water on his head, holding in his right hand a standard. The fifth shows a cupboard open and shelved in the middle—above is a chalice and paten, below is a salver with fruit within and falling from it. The sixth contains an organ case with a man who, with raised head, enjoys the sweetness of the sounds, on the side of the organ are the arms of the Opera and below are the arms of the rector Arringhieri. The seventh is a cupboard half open with pierced doors, in the upper half a censer, and an incense boat, with a label above with these words, 'Dirigatur Domine oratio mea sicut incensum in conspectu tuo.' Below is the holy water pot with the sprinkler within, and with a pair of sacrament cruets. The eighth shows the figure of a man with a glory and a diadem on his head, with face and right arm raised to heaven, representing whom I do not understand; above him is a garden full of different flowers and trees. The ninth is a cupboard cut across and half open; in the upper part a label with these words 'Qui post me venit, ante me factus est. Cujus non sum dignus calceamente solvere;' below are different musical instruments, the words above are set to plain song. The tenth, that is the centre one, is a half-length of S. John Baptist with the cross in his left hand, and in the right a label with the words, 'Ecce Agnus Dei,' while with his finger he points to Christ in a figure which represents him. The eleventh shows another cupboard half open and shelved, above is a label on which are some lines of the hymn of S. John Baptist, with notes in plain song and with the name of the author above, which was Alessandro Agricola, and below is a flute and a violin with its bow. The twelfth is the figure of a young man with a label below which says, 'Johannis Baptistæ discipulus.' This is generally thought to represent S. Andrew the apostle. The thirteenth is another open cupboard with a shelf. In the upper part is a chalice and more fruit, and in the lower a hollow dish with a foot also full of fruit. The fourteenth shows the half-length of a man who plays a lute, above him appears a garden with different trees. The fifteenth is a cupboard with open division, with a little gate and grating with almond shaped openings, above is a candlestick with a candle half burnt, and below is a box full of yellow tapers. The sixteenth represents S. Catherine with her wheel, half-length, disputing with the tyrant, before her is an open book on which are cut these words, 'Catharina disputationis virginitatis ac martirii palmam reportat.' The seventeenth shows a cupboard divided and half closed, with a grating like the others, above is a missal laid down, with a chalice upright, and a paten on the missal, and there are also a pair of spectacles and another paten leaning against the wall, below there is a closed book which seems to be a breviary, upon which is an open book with these words, 'Ecce mitto angelum meum ante faciem tuam, qui preparabit viam tuam ante te. Vox clamantis in deserto; parate viam Domini: rectas facite semitas ejus.' The eighteenth shows a fine gate through which one sees a garden, within which appear different trees with fruit on them, and at the bottom is a little table upon which is an inkstand with a pen and a penknife with a label which issues from the inkstand with these words, 'Alberto Aringherio operaio fabre factum.' The last panel shows an open cupboard with shelf and grating, above is a harp and below is a violin and other musical instruments. The rector Arringhieri paid 4090 scudi for the work as a matter of compromise on the valuing of Fra Giovanni da Verona. It was in so dark a place that it could not be seen except with lighted torches, and it was also damaged because it was put in a newly built place, the walls of which were not sufficiently dry to receive such delicate work." This account was written in 1786.

[3] The panel illustrated from the Albert and Victoria Museum is a good average specimen of this kind, but not quite a masterpiece.

[4] In 1453 Matteo di Giovanni Bartoli, painter, says that he possesses the half of certain tools and appliances of his art, which are not worth 20 florins, and that the other half belongs to Giovanni di Pietro, painter, his partner. That they are in a house or dwelling that they hire from Guicciardo Forteguerri in the Palazzo Forteguerri, which they have as a house and not a shop, and that he has nothing else in the world but a few debts

(!). He says that he makes no profit, but is learning as well as he can, and that his uncle, Ser Francescho di Bartolo, the notary, keeps him. This is a young and promising artist who cannot get on. Priamo della Quercia, brother of the celebrated sculptor Jacopo della Fonte, painter, says that he is poor and without anything to live on; that he has a girl of marriageable age and a young boy; that he owes money to several people. He had a dower of 200 florins which came from a possession which the nuns of Ogni Santi held, because they said that they were heirs to his daughter-in-law, a nun in that convent (!) and they had kept possession for six years and he could not sue these nuns at law on account of his poverty. There are several documents referring to money and property which his brother left to this man, but which he seems to have difficulty in obtaining possession of, and he gives one the impression of being unfortunate through life. In the same year Antonio di Ser Naddo, painter, says he has a house with an oven within the walls of Siena, "male in ponto," in which he lives in the Contrada of Camporegi. That he has three useless mouths in the house which gain nothing, two children, one a boy, and the other a girl of marriageable age, but if he dowered her, so that she could be married, he would have nothing to live on. Also that he owes 20 florins to various people. In the same year others, both painters and woodworkers, complain that they have nothing to live on and owe money, some saying that they have become old and poor in the art. In 1478 Ventura di Ser Giuliano, architect and woodcarver, says that he has a little house in the city division in the place called of S.

Salvador, and that he is away at Naples because of his debts, for he is afraid to return. That he owes Ser Biagio, the priest, 80 florins and other persons 402. In 1488 Giovanni di Cristofano Ghini, painter, says that he has a vineyard at Terraia in the commune of S. Giorgio a Papaino from which he receives in dues about 24 florins. That he has a wife and three sons and nothing to keep them on. That five years ago he had sold all that he had in the house, for times were very bad. That though he sticks to his work so closely that he does not even go for a walk he has not made the bread which he has eaten in the last six years. That he and his father have to keep a sister who was married to Andreoccio d'Andrea di Pizichino with her three little sons unless they are to die of hunger, and that they have a girl of marriageable age in the house, his sister, "Che è il fiorimento d'ognichosa." In the same year Benvenuto di Giovanni says that he is obliged to work away from Siena because his gains are so small; and finally in 1521, Ventura di Ser Giuliano di Tura petitions the Balia as follows:—He was a master joiner and says that he passed his youth and almost all his age in gathering ancient objects and carvings, which the craftsmen of the city have copied, so that one may say that the antique in the city has been re-discovered by his labours. But that he has not by this benefit to the craftsmen provided for his old age, since both he and his wife have been very unwell for years past, and that he finds himself old, with four little daughters, "one no heavier than the other," so he asks for a little pension of eight lire a month (which has been suspended apparently), so that he may not have to go to the hospital for bread with his wife and the four little ones.

CPSIA information can be obtained at www.ICGtesting.com
Printed in the USA
LVOW11s1652030815

448642LV00002B/277/P